I Need The Light

26 Weekly Devotionals to Help You Through Winter

JANET MORRISON

Contents

Sources Used in This Book   VII

Introduction   XI

1. Let There Be Light   1
   Genesis 1:1-5

2. A Lamp to My Feet   7
   Psalm 119:105

3. The People Will See a Great Light   11
   Isaiah 9:1-2

4. John the Baptist   17
   John 1:6-8

5. Jesus is The Real Thing   23
   John 1:9

6. The People Will See a Great Light   31
   Matthew 4:12-17

7. Y'all Are the Light of the World   37
Matthew 5:13-16

8. He is a Light to Reveal God to the Nations   47
Luke 2:32

9. Your Body Fills with Light   53
Matthew 6:22-23

10. No One Lights a Lamp then Hides It   63
Luke 8:16-18

11. It Bears Repeating, No One Lights a Lamp then Hides It   69
Luke 11:33-36

12. Parable of the Lost Coin   75
Luke 15:8

13. The Word was the Source of Life and This Life Brought Light to Mankind   81
John 1:4

14. The Life-Light Blazed Out of the Darkness; the Darkness Couldn't Put it Out   87
John 1:5

15. People Working and Living in Truth Welcome God-Light   93
John 3:19-21

16. The Light of the World   103
John 8:12

17. Those Who Walk in the Dark Don't Know Where They're Going   109
John 12:35-36

18. I Came as a Light so No One Who Believes in Me 113
  Should Stay in Darkness
  John 12:46

19. Paul on the Road to Damascus 117
  Acts 9:1-9

20. Let Light Shine Out of Darkness 125
  II Corinthians 4:1-6

21. We Don't Belong to the Darkness 133
  I Thessalonians 5:5

22. Brought Life and Immortality to Light Through the 137
  Gospel
  II Timothy 1:10

23. Chosen People... Out of Darkness into a Wonderful 143
  Light
  I Peter 2:9-10

24. Every Perfect Gift... From the Father of Light and lights 147
  James 1:16-17

25. If We Walk in Light,... Christ... Cleans Us from All Sin 151
  I John 1:5

26. God is Light 155
  I John 1:6-10

27. My Prayer for You 161

28. Recipe Index 165

29. About the author 167

30. Also by Janet Morrison 169

Sources Used in This Book

The Acts of the Apostles, by Barclay   William Barclay, *The Acts of the Apostles, Revised Edition* (Westminster John Knox Press, 1976).

Good News Bible   English, Bible. *Today's Good News Bible: The Bible in Today's English Version*, 1976.

The Gospel of Matthew, by Barclay   Barclay, William. *The Gospel of Matthew, Volume One, Revised Edition: Chapters 1-32* (Westminster John Knox Press, 1975).

Halley's Bible Handbook   Henry H. Halley, *Halley's Bible Handbook: An Abbreviated Bible Commentary*, 1964.

The Layman's Bible Commentary, Vol II Isaiah by Wright   Wright, B. Ernest. Layman, *Layman's Bible Commentary: Vol II Isaiah*, 1963.

The Layman's Bible Commentary, Vol. 19 John, by Wright
Wright, B. Ernest. Layman, *Layman's Bible Commentary: Vol. 19 John*, 1963.

The Letters of James and Peter, by Barclay   Barclay, William. *The Letters of James and Peter, Revised Edition* (Westminster John Knox Press, 1976).

The Letters of John and Jude, by Barclay   Barclay, William. *The Letters of John and Jude, Revised Edition* (Westminster John Knox Press, 1975).

The Letters to the Philippians, Colossians, and Thessalonians, by Barclay   Barclay, William. *The Letters to the Philippians, Colossians, and Thessalonians, Revised Edition* (Westminster John Knox Press, 1975).

The Letters to Timothy, Titus, and Philemon, by Barclay
Barclay, William. *The Letters to Timothy, Titus, and Philemon, Revised Edition* (Westminster John Knox Press, 1975).

The Living Bible   Tyndale House Publishers, *The Living Bible, Paraphrased* (Tyndale House Publishers, 1971).

Matthew For Everyone, Part 1   Wright, N.T. *Matthew For Everyone, Part 1* (Westminster John Knox Press, 2002)

The Message   Eugene H. Peterson, *The Message: The Bible in Contemporary Language* (Tyndale House, 2005).

New Oxford Annotated Bible   Oxford University Press et al., *New Oxford Annotated Bible*, 1991.

NIV Study Bible   Zondervan, *NIV Study Bible, Fully Revised Edition* (Zondervan, 2020).

The Psalms of David, in Metre   *The Psalms of David, in Metre* (Philadelphia: William S. Young, 1849).

Reading the Bible with Rabbi Jesus   Lois Tverberg, *Reading the Bible with Rabbi Jesus: How a Jewish Perspective Can Transform Your Understanding (Baker Books, 2018).*

Sitting at the Feet of Rabbi Jesus   Ann Spangler and Lois Tverberg, *Sitting at the Feet of Rabbi Jesus: How the Jewishness of Jesus Can Transform Your Faith. Zondervan, 2018.*

The TouchPoint Bible   Tyndale House Publishers, *The TouchPoint Bible,* 1996.

Walking in the Dust of Rabbi Jesus   Lois Tverberg, *Walking in the Dust of Rabbi Jesus: How the Jewish Words of Jesus Can Change Your Life* (Zondervan, 2012).

Introduction

Winter has always been my least favorite season. I have had Chronic Fatigue Syndrome (CFS)/Myalgic Encephalomyelitis (ME) since 1987 and Fibromyalgia since soon thereafter. These are year-round conditions, but they are made worse by cold temperatures and sudden changes in the weather.

A few years ago, I was diagnosed with Seasonal Affective Disorder (SAD). My physician's assistant urged me to get outside in the early- to mid-morning to soak in the natural light to ease my SAD symptoms. I have had limited success because I am not a "morning person" and in cool and cold weather I have the added body aches due to CFS/ME and Fibromyalgia.

Fibromyalgia exacerbates my dislike of cold weather. In the autumn and winter months I often wake up in the morning in the fetal position with my fingers curled into my palms. I am stiff all over and have almost constant pain in my neck and head. This pain sometimes permeates into my gums. After 38 years of this illness, it is just a part of the life I have accepted.

I have a lower-than-normal core body temperature. My body, therefore, concentrates its heat around my essential organs. This results in limited heat for my hands and feet. They are cold for six months of the year.

I do not seek your sympathy for any of these maladies. I mention them in this introduction merely to explain what my experience has been and to let others who suffer with any of these issues know that they are not alone.

Everybody has something. Illness and mental challenges are a part of life. Jesus never promised us a life without pain, sorrow, grief, or frustration. He promised to be here with us.

This devotional book grew out of my experience.

As I walked one cold morning, I had to will my feet to keep stepping forward. In an effort to get into a rhythm and remind myself why I was walking on such a cold day, I repeated over and over the words, "I need the light. I need the light." It was on around the fifth repetition that "light" (lowercase) became "Light" (capitalized.)

I needed sunlight on my face to combat the seasonal tendency I have not to be joyful in the fall and winter months. The light my face needs for SAD is the lowercase "light." The capitalized "Light" my soul — my whole being — needs is Jesus Christ.

I had the idea to write a book highlighting some of the times and ways in which "light" and "Light" appear in the Bible to illustrate my need for both light and Light. It was as I was studying Matthew 5:14-16 that a "lightbulb" came on in my head and I realized there is a third part to the equation: God has given me an assignment. I am to be a light to the world!

I need sunlight in the mornings to overcome SAD.

I need the Lord Jesus Christ in all aspects of my being because He is my Rock. He is my Salvation. He overcame death for me. He overcame death for you.

I need to be light — to be a light — to shine God's Light for others to see, to reflect His Light and not keep Him a secret.

God has made me a light-bearer. He has put me on a hilltop and a light stand and He expects me to be generous with His Light.

I have no formal religious training. I grew up in the Presbyterian denomination and am a member of a congregation affiliated with the Presbyterian Church, USA. I have written this devotional book as a layperson.

I am not an "in your face" kind of Christian, so I stepped out of my comfort zone to write this devotional book. If you are looking for a book that scares you into being a Christian, this book is not for you.

You might prefer to read versions of the Bible that I have not included in this book. You might not agree with all my statements or all the statements I have quoted from other sources.

I selected 26 Scripture passages about light or The Light. After studying those passages in five versions of the Bible, I arranged them in the order that made sense to me and decided to present them as 26 weekly devotionals.

Winter is not 26 weeks long but, if you are like me, your Seasonal Affective Disorder or increased pain from fibromyalgia sets in around the first of September here in the northern hemisphere and hangs on until the daytime temperatures reach the 70s F. That is about 26 weeks, or half the year.

Some of the weekly devotionals include a section called "My Thoughts." Those are the weeks that the Scripture passage either especially spoke to me or sparked questions or deeper thinking in my mind. Each devotional includes a sentence to remember, a thought pattern interrupter to help you combat negative thoughts, a suggested activity, and a recipe for a dish I find comforting. Most of the devotionals include insights from commentaries written by Rev. William Barclay.

Rev. William Barclay was a Presbyterian minister in Scotland. He wrote a series of commentaries covering the entire Protestant Bible. My mother relied heavily on Barclay's books and H.H. Halley's book, *Halley's Bible Handbook* as she taught Bible lessons and Sunday School for many years. I inherited her reliance on those resources.

The thought pattern interrupters are suggested for you to consider to counteract any negative thoughts you are having due to the season.

The recipes are some of my favorite cold weather foods. They all fall into the category of "comfort foods." I hope you will find comfort and warmth in the ones you choose to make.

It is my prayer that whether or not you have Seasonal Affective Disorder or physical conditions that make the cooler months of the year challenging, that you will find these 26 devotionals helpful in your daily journey.

Janet Morrison

Let There Be Light

Setting the stage: The Book of Genesis is the first book in the Bible, so it is only fitting that it begins with a story of creation. The verses for this week are, therefore, the first five verses in the Bible. The first thing God created out of the black emptiness was light.

This story of creation is presented as a six-day process plus the seventh day on which God rested. Science tells us that the creation of the world and all its wonders took hundreds of millions of years. For me, that takes nothing away from the creation story in the first chapter of Genesis. The point is that God created everything out of nothing by the power of His word. It doesn't matter to me whether He did it in six days or six billion years.

Genesis 1:1-5, as written in *The Message:* "First this: God created the Heavens and Earth — all you see, all you don't see. Earth was a soup of nothingness, a bottomless emptiness, an inky blackness. God's

Spirit brooded like a bird above the watery abyss. God spoke: 'Light!'
And light appeared. God saw that light was good and separated light
from dark. God named the light Day, he named the dark Night. It was
evening, it was morning — Day One."

Genesis 1:1-5, as written in *The Good News Bible:* "In the
beginning, when God created the universe, the earth was engulfed
in total darkness, and the power of God was moving over the water.
Then God commanded, 'Let there be light' —and light appeared.
God was pleased with what he saw. Then he separated the light from
the darkness, and he named the light 'Day' and the darkness 'Night.'
Evening passed and morning came — that was the first day."

Genesis 1:1-5, as written in *The Living Bible:* "When God began creating the heavens and the earth, the earth was at first a shapeless,
chaotic mass, with the Spirit of God brooding over the dark vapors.
Then God said, 'Let there be light.' And light appeared. And God
was pleased with it, and divided the light from the darkness. So he let it
shine for awhile, and then there was darkness again. He called the light
'daytime,' and the darkness 'nighttime.' Together they formed the first
day."

**Genesis 1:1-5, as written in *The New Oxford Annotated
Bible (NRSV):*** "In the beginning when God created the heavens and
the earth, the earth was a formless void and darkness covered the face
of the deep, while a wind from God swept over the face of the water.
Then God said, 'Let there be light'; and there was light. And God saw
that the light was good; and God separated the light from the darkness.
God called the light Day and the darkness he called Night. And there
was evening and there was morning, the first day."

A footnote in *The New Oxford Annotated Bible (NRSV)* for verses 3-5 points out that "Light burst forth first (2 Corinthians 4:6), even before the creation of the sun (vv. 14-18), and was *separated* from *night*, a remnant of uncreated darkness (v. 2). Since the Jewish day began with sundown, the order is *evening* and *morning*."

Genesis 1:1-5, as written in *TouchPoint Bible:* "In the beginning God created the heavens and the earth. The earth was empty, a formless mass cloaked in darkness. And the Spirit of God was hovering over its surface. Then God said, 'Let there be light,' and there was light. And God saw that it was good. Then he separated the light from the darkness. God called the light 'day' and the darkness 'night.' Together these made up one day."

My thoughts: Even though I've heard and read the first chapter of Genesis many times, until I read that footnote in *The New Oxford Annotated Bible (NRSV),* I had not realized that when God said, "Let there be light" it was not the sun being created. The creation of the sun, moon, and stars comes in verses 14-18, on the fourth day.

Can you imagine living in total darkness? I can't. Likewise, I can't imagine being without some darkness.

In elementary school, we learned about "The Land of the Midnight Sun." It was intriguing and thousands of miles from North Carolina. It might as well have been on another planet because I couldn't wrap my head around such a concept.

It wasn't until I visited the northernmost tip of the Isle of Lewis in the Outer Hebrides of Scotland a few summers ago that I sort of experienced "the midnight sun." It was light enough until 11:00 p.m. to see to read outdoors, and by 3:00 a.m. the sun had risen. It was wonderful as a tourist, but I think if I had 20 hours of daylight every day for weeks on end every summer, I would soon work myself to death.

On the flip side, I understand that in those parts of Scotland there are winter days when the sun rises around 9:00 a.m. and sets around 3:00 p.m. Having Seasonal Affective Disorder in the fall and winter, I know I wouldn't like that schedule. I imagine it would magnify one's fibromyalgia aches and pains as well. I suppose whatever climate and latitude you are used to would have an effect on how your body responds to the amount of light and darkness you experience in a day.

Remember: God created light by the power of His word.

Thought Pattern Interrupter: Don't miss the beauty of fall by dreading winter.

Activity Suggestion: Buy a Christmas cactus or plant flower bulbs. Or, inquire at your local public library about book clubs in your area. Join one!

Comfort Recipe: Mama's Drop Biscuits

This is one of my favorite comfort foods, but I rarely make biscuits in the summer. I don't want to heat up the kitchen by using the oven.

My mother didn't have a written recipe for her drop biscuits, but she was kind enough to guesstimate a recipe for me when I got my first apartment. After years of making biscuits, like her, I don't need the written recipe anymore.

- 2 cups self-rising flour

- 1/3 cup shortening

- Milk

Mix together the flour and shortening with a pastry blender or fork. Add enough milk to make a soft dough. Stir only until flour is moistened. Drop by spoonful on greased pan. Bake at 450 degrees F. until golden brown, about 12 minutes.

Slice the biscuits open as soon as they are cool enough not to burn your fingers and stick a pat of butter between the two halves. Yum!

Yield: 6-8 biscuits, depending on how big you like your biscuits. That also affects baking time, but check on the biscuits after about 10 minutes.

A Lamp to My Feet

Setting the stage: God's Spirit shines through the hymns Christians sing, and many of them are based on Psalms. The Psalter, or Book of Psalms, dates to ancient Israel. The Psalms serve both Jewish and Christian believers. The 119th Psalm contains 22 stanzas of eight lines each for a total of 176 verses. Although it is thought that David wrote more than half of the 150 Psalms, scholars believe Psalm 119 was written later by more than one person.

In *Walking in the Dust of Rabbi Jesus: How the Jewish Words of Jesus Can Change Your Life*, scholar and author Lois Tverberg advises modern-day Bible readers to keep in mind that what is typically translated in the Bible as "law," Jews more correctly understand as "guidance" or "teaching." As will be mentioned in several chapters of this devotional book, there are nuances in the languages in which the Scriptures were originally written that lose something when translated into English.

Psalm 119:105, as written in *The Message:* "By your words I can see where I'm going, they throw a beam of light on my dark path."

Psalm 119:105, as written in *The Good News Bible:* "Your word is a lamp to guide me and a light for my path."

Psalm 119:105, as written in *The Living Bible:* "Your words are a flashlight to light the path ahead of me, and keep me from stumbling." (If you live in the United Kingdom, you might want to substitute "torch" for "flashlight" in this version.)

Psalm 119:105, as written in *The New Oxford Annotated Bible (NRSV)*: "Your word is a lamp to my feet and a light to my path."

Psalm 119:105, as written in *TouchPoint Bible:* "Your word is a lamp for my feet and a light for my path."

Psalm 119:105, as written in *The Psalms of David, in Metre (1849)*: "Thy word is to my feet a lamp, and to my path a light."

My thoughts: This verse is straightforward. It describes the Bible — the Word of God — as a lamp to light our way in life. Just as I need light to ease my Seasonal Affective Disorder in the fall and winter, I need the Bible as my roadmap on my journey through life. I need the light, and I need The Light.

Remember: The Bible will always light my way.

Thought Pattern Interrupter: God must have had a good reason to create winter.

Activity Suggestion: You know that winter coat, jacket, or sweater that you can no longer wear or no longer need? Take it to a thrift shop or homeless shelter so it can bring warmth and joy to someone else.

Comfort Recipe: Mary Jane's Meatloaf

This makes a large meatloaf, but that's a positive thing. Let it cool or even chill the leftovers, then slice it, and freeze in individual slices for meals in the future. Those slices make great meatloaf sandwiches! This was a recipe of my mother's friend, Mary Jane Phillips McCachren.

- 2 pounds ground beef

- 1 small raw potato, grated

- 1 small onion, chopped

- 1 cup corn flakes, crushed

- 3/4 cup ketchup

- 2 eggs

- 1/2 teaspoon salt

- Dash of black pepper, or to your taste

Mix all ingredients together. Form into a loaf and put in a foil-lined 7x11-inch baking dish. Bake at 375 degrees F. for 1 hour, or a little longer to make sure the center is well-done.

Yield: Will serve 8 to 10 persons or more.

The People Will See a Great Light

Scripture for this week: Isaiah 9:1-2

Setting the stage: The main point of this Scripture passage is, of course, The Light; however, it refers to the tribes of Zebulun and Naphtali, which meant nothing to me. I turned to *The Layman's Bible Commentary, Vol. 11, The Book of Isaiah*, by B. Ernest Wright, for the following background information:

"This historical reference to the land of the tribes of Zebulun and Naphtali is to be understood in connection with the campaign of Tiglath-pilser III in 733 B.C. which took away from Israel all of Galilee; the last phrase should be understood as referring to the course of the highway 'from the land beyond the Jordan to Galilee of the nations.' In the days to come Galilee will be restored and made glorious. The implication of the verse is that while Galilee had been removed from Israel by the Assyrians, Samaria itself had not yet fallen as it was to do between 724 and 721 B.C."

Also, King Ahaz was a weak king in 734 B.C., which could be seen as a time of darkness. It was an opportune time for God to use the prophet Isaiah to remind the Jews that He would bring forth a king (Jesus Christ) to fulfill His promises.

Isaiah 9:1-2, as written in *The Message:* "But there'll be no darkness for those who were in trouble. Earlier he did bring the lands of Zebulun and Naphtali into disrepute, but the time is coming when he'll make that whole area glorious — the road along the Sea, the country past the Jordan, international Galilee. The people who walked in darkness have seen a great light. For those who lived in a land of deep shadows — light! Sunbursts of light!"

Isaiah 9:1-2, as written in *The Good News Bible:* "The land of the tribes of Zebulun and Naphtali was once disgraced, but the future will bring honor to this region, from the Mediterranean eastward to the land on the other side of the Jordan, and even in Galilee itself, where the foreigners live. The people who walked in darkness have seen a great light. They lived in a land of shadows, but now light is shining on them."

Isaiah 9:1-2, as written in *The Living Bible:* "Nevertheless, that time of darkness and despair shall not go on forever. Though soon the land of Zebulun and Naphtali will be under God's contempt and judgment, yet in the future these very lands, Galilee and Northern Transjordan, where lies the road to the sea, will be filled with glory. The people who walk in darkness shall see a great Light — a Light that will shine on all those who live in the land of the shadow of death."

Isaiah 9:1-2, as written in *The New Oxford Annotated Bible (NRSV)*: "But there will be no gloom for those who were in anguish. In the former time he brought into contempt the land of Zebulun and the land of Naphtali, but in the latter time he will make glorious the way of the sea, the land beyond the Jordan, Galilee of the nations. The people who walked in darkness have seen a great light; those who lived in a land of deep darkness — on them light has shined."

Isaiah 9:1-2, as written in *TouchPoint Bible:* In words very much like those in *The Living Bible,* "Nevertheless, that time of darkness and despair will not go on forever. The land of Zebulun and Naphtali will soon be humbled, but there will be a time in the future when Galilee of the Gentiles, which lies along the road that runs between Jordan and the sea, will be filled with glory. The people who walk in darkness will see a great light — a light that will shine on all who live in the land where death casts its shadow."

My thoughts: Those verses from Isaiah are repeated in Matthew 4:15-16 in a Scripture about Jesus beginning to preach when He heard that John the Baptist had been arrested.

I wrote the first draft of this devotional book in the early months of 2023. When I sat down to read and edit the book, the Israel-Gaza War of 2023 was in its fifth week. It is interesting how current events can and often do influence how we read a passage of Scripture. I am reminded that the State of Israel, which was created after World War II, should not be confused with Israel of the Old Testament. The State of Israel today is a specific geographical area and a country formed on May 14, 1948. The League of Nations adopted the British map of Israel in 1922, but the country's borders have been in dispute ever since. Palestinians see the land as theirs for an independent Palestine and Jews see the land as theirs. The history of the land is, of course, centuries old and I am not qualified to encapsulate it here. That is not the purpose of this devotional book. If you want to know more, I recommend that you read reliable source materials on the subject.

Just as Isaiah told the people of Zebulun and Naphtali they were going to see a great light (i.e., Jesus Christ), you must try to find the good, the positive things about the cold months of the year. I am saying that to myself. I know it is hard to do.

I'm addressing those comments to myself as well as to you. I tend to say, "I hate winter,: or "I hate cold weather, or "I always feel worse mentally and physically in the fall and winter." I cannot let that become a self-fulfilling prophecy!

Remember: God always keeps His promises.

Thought Pattern Interrupter: I'm not weird just because I dread winter.

Activity Suggestion: Clean out a closet. Put aside items to donate to someone or an organization.

Comfort Recipe: Barbecue Stacks

This is super simple, especially if you have the ingredients pre-measured or even frozen (except for maybe the cheese) in advance.

Per person:

- 1/4 to 1/3 cup chopped barbecue pork

- 2 frozen hash brown potato patties

- 1 slice of Swiss cheese, cut in half (or grated Swiss cheese)

Preheat oven or toaster oven to 450 degrees F. (or the temperature designated for the brand of hash brown patties you're using.)

Multiply the listed ingredients by the number of servings needed.

For each serving, place one frozen hash brown potato patty on a baking sheet. Place half a slice of Swiss cheese or a desired amount of grated Swiss cheese on top of it. Spoon the chopped barbecue on top of the cheese. Place the other half-slice of cheese or more grated Swiss cheese on top of the barbecue. Place the other frozen hash brown potato patty on top of the cheese.

Bake the stack(s) for approximately half the baking time indicated for the brand of hash brown patties you're using. When that time is up, remove the baking sheet from the oven and carefully flip the stack(s) over. Put back in the oven and bake until patties are golden brown on top.

John the Baptist

Setting the stage: This Scripture passage introduces John the Baptist to us.

John 1:6-8, as written in *The Message:* "There once was a man, his name was John, sent by God to point out the way of the Life-Light. He came to show everyone where to look, who to believe in. John was not himself the Light; he was there to show the way to the Light."

John 1:6-8, as written in *The Good News Bible:* "God sent his messenger, a man named John, who came to tell people about the light, so that all should hear the message and believe. John himself was not the Light; he was only a witness to identify it."

John 1:6-8, as written in *The Living Bible:* "God sent John the Baptist as a witness to the fact that Jesus Christ is the true Light. John himself was not the Light; he was only a witness to identify it."

The emphasis in this paraphrased version is not on who John the Baptist was sent to tell. The word that jumps out at me in this version is "fact." John the Baptist and the author of The Gospel of John (the writer of The Gospel of John being one of the 12 disciples of Jesus) both knew that it was a fact that Jesus was <u>The</u> <u>Light</u>. It wasn't just John the disciple's opinion.

John 1:6-8, as written in *The New Oxford Annotated Bible (NRSV)*: "John (the Baptist), climaxing the Old Testament prophets, was *sent* (commissioned by God, Malachi 3:1) to point to Jesus (vv. 19-34).

The parentheticals are part of the quote; I added nothing except to spell out "Malachi" which was abbreviated in the original.

John 1:6-8, as written in *TouchPoint Bible:* "God sent John the Baptist to tell everyone about the light so that everyone might believe because of his testimony. John himself was not the light; he was only a witness to the light."

Like in *The Message* and *The Living Bible*, the emphasis is on "everyone." God was sending Jesus Christ to save everyone. John the Baptist was sent to tell everyone that Jesus was not just coming but Jesus was already here.

This passage is straightforward, but let's see what a Bible commentary says about it.

***The Gospel of John, Vol. 1*, by William Barclay:** William Barclay tells us that some people put John the Baptist up on a pedestal, so to speak. They elevated him to a position higher than they should have, so John 1:8 reminds us that John the Baptist is a witness or messenger and not The Light himself.

Barclay writes, "There are, in fact, indications that there was actually a sect who put John the Baptist in the highest place. We find an echo of them in Acts 19:3-4. In Ephesus Paul came upon certain people who knew nothing but the baptism of John."

Barclay goes on to explain that the writer of The Gospel of John was not criticizing John the Baptist; he was just warning us not to put John the Baptist in "a place that encroached upon the place of Jesus Himself." This is a point that is repeated throughout John's Gospel.

In fact, in John 1:20, we see John the Baptist denying that he is Christ or even a great prophet. The writer of John knew there was a tendency for people in the church to give John the Baptist a higher place than they should. Barclay cautions us, "It can still happen that men may worship a preacher rather than Christ."

We've seen this all too often in our own time. There are preachers and televangelists who are elevated to the point that their followers lose sight of God and Jesus Christ.

John 1:8 cautions laypeople and preachers alike to guard against any confusion between the messenger and the Message, between the lamp and The Light, between the witness and The Light.

My thoughts: Something that jumped out at me in this passage in *The Message* were the words, "where to look." That angle is not expressed in that way in any of the other versions. Ponder that for a minute. John the Baptist tells us where to look.

Verse 6 in the first chapter of John's Gospel introduces John the Baptist but quickly moves on to Jesus Christ, The Light. John the Baptist came not to draw attention to himself but to point people to Jesus Christ.

Perhaps, the most important thing we can take from John 1:6-8 is that our lives, too, should point to Jesus. Are we not called to bear witness?

Remember: Like John the Baptist, we are messengers for Jesus Christ.

Thought Pattern Interrupter: I will embrace the blessings of winter.

Activity Suggestion: Make a list of the blessings of winter. At least, try. Then invite a friend to go out for lunch. Or, if you live alone, invite friends over for dinner and try the recipe below.

Comfort Recipe: Easy Cheesy Lasagna

- 1 pound ground beef

- 26-oz. jar spaghetti sauce

- 8-oz. pkg. wide egg noodles, cooked

- 8-oz. pkg. shredded mozzarella cheese

- 1 cup cottage cheese

- 1 cup grated Parmesan cheese

Brown ground beef; drain. Stir spaghetti sauce into the beef and simmer for several minutes. Add the cooked noodles, mozzarella cheese, and cottage cheese. Mix well and transfer to a greased 2-quart baking dish. Sprinkle the Parmesan cheese on top.

Bake at 350 degrees F. for 30 minutes.

Yield: 4-6 servings, depending on appetites.

Jesus is The Real Thing

S cripture for this week: John 1:9

Setting the stage: Just because this week's passage is only one verse, don't be fooled. Get ready to dig deeper. There is a lot to unpack here! This one verse can prompt a lot of thoughts and questions. You might want to reread the Scripture for Week 4, John 1:6-8.

John 1:9, as written in *The Message:* "The Life-Light was the real thing: Every person entering Life he brings into Light."

John 1:9, as written in *The Good News Bible:* "This was the real thing — the light that comes into the world and shines on all mankind."

This brings to mind the old Coca-Cola slogan: "It's the real thing." John 1:9 is telling us that Jesus is the real thing. He is the Christ.

He is the Messiah. He is the One who comes on Earth and shines on everyone — on all mankind.

"Mankind" is an interesting word and perhaps it was carefully chosen by the writers of this version of the Bible.

When I looked up the definition of mankind, just as I expected, I found that it means the human race. It doesn't just mean those people alive now; it doesn't mean just those people alive when Jesus walked on the Earth in human form. Jesus shines on all the human race from the beginning of the world to the very end of the future. All humans.

Why is that definition of "mankind" important? It is not only inclusive of all people hearing or reading the teachings of Jesus. Does it not include all people from the beginning of time? Or am I going down a misguided rabbit hole? In case you have ever wondered what happens to the people who lived before Jesus walked the Earth in human form or the people who never had the opportunity to hear about Jesus, *The Message* seems to be saying they were and are somehow taken care of. That's not to say everyone will be saved. God gave humans free will. Some people will reject him.

For instance, a good friend of mine was Jewish. Before she died she said to me, "I wish I had what you have. How do I get it?" I told her all she had to do was accept Jesus Christ as her Lord and Savior. She asked if my pastor at the time, the Rev. Dr. Kyle Hite, would talk to her. Kyle, of course, gladly did. I do not know anything about their conversation. I don't know if she accepted Christ before she died, but the words in *The Message* give me hope that she has had another opportunity.

But worrying about my friend's soul for eternity is not the point of John 1:9. The point of John 1:9 is for the reader or hearer to understand that Jesus Christ is the Savior.

John 1:9, as written in *The Living Bible*: "Later on, the one who is the true Light arrived to shine on everyone coming into the world."

John has been talking about John the Baptist in the previous verses. In verse 9 he is making a distinction between John the Baptist and Jesus Christ. Jesus is the true Light and He came to shine on everyone coming into the world. He didn't come for a chosen few. He came to save everyone.

John 1:9, as written in *The New Oxford Annotated Bible (NRSV)*: "The true light, which enlightens everyone, was coming into the world."

Here we have "the true light" and it is the light "which enlightens everyone...."

The footnote for verse 9 in *The New Oxford Annotated Bible* states, "*True light* is real, underived light, contrasted not with false light, but with those such as John, who was but a lamp (5:35)."

What struck me in the footnote was the word *underived*. Jesus was the source of light. Although it's a different kind of light, it's like the sun compared to the moon. Without the sun, the moon would have no light. The moon reflects the sun's light, just as we are supposed to reflect the Light of Jesus Christ.

In the footnote there is another reference to John the Baptist. He was a lamp casting a light on Jesus. Is that not what God calls us to do?

John 1:9, as written in *TouchPoint Bible*: "The one who is the true light, who gives light to everyone, was going to come into the world."

Let's see what a Bible commentary says about it.

The Gospel of John, Vol. 1, **by William Barclay:** Rev. Barclay gives this verse more than two pages. He begins by pointing out that by saying Jesus was the *real* light, John used a significant word.

In the following paragraph, there is a quote from *The Gospel of John, Vol. 1*, by Barclay. He was a product of the early 20th century and, therefore, did not use inclusive language. When he says "men," substitute "people" in your head. If you are not a male, you're used to having to do that.

Barclay explains that there are two words that are similar. *Alēthēs* means true as in a statement being true. "*Alēthinos* means *real* or *genuine* as opposed to unreal. So what John is saying is that Jesus is the real light come to enlighten and to illumine men. Before Jesus came there were other lights which men followed. Some were flickers of the truth; some were faint glimpses of reality; some were will o' the wisps which men followed, and which led men out into the dark and left them there. It is still the case.... Jesus is the only genuine light, the real light to guide men on their way."

Barclay goes on to compare the coming of Jesus to a flash of lightning in the pitch black of night that illuminates everything. "His coming dissipated the shadows of *doubt*. Until He came men could only guess about God."

Think of a time when you experienced a severe thunderstorm at night — a storm punctuated by vivid bolts of lightning that lit up the entire sky and, perhaps, even the inside of your home. Until you experienced that, you did not have a complete grasp of what such a storm was like.

Likewise, until Jesus Christ came to Earth in human form, people could not really grasp or understand the love and greatness of God.

Also from Barclay, "His coming dissipated the shadows of *despair.... Jesus came to a world that was in despair....* Men despaired of ever making themselves or the world what they knew they and it ought to be. But with the coming of Jesus a new power, a new dynamic came into life. He came not only with knowledge but with power. He came not only to show men the right way but to enable them to walk in it.... The darkness of pessimism and despair were gone for ever."

Barclay also wrote: "His coming dissipated the darkness of *death*. The ancient world feared death.... But Jesus by His coming, by His life, His death, His Resurrection showed men that death was only the way to a larger life. The darkness of death was gone."

We have no reason to fear death today because Jesus Christ came to Earth and died for our sins 2,000 years ago. We might dread or even fear sickness and suffering (or the coming of winter), but we need not fear death. Our ancient ancestors had no such reassurance that they would be all right in the afterlife.

Barclay goes on to remind us that in the ancient world Jews hated Gentiles, Greeks thought knowledge was reserved for the few, and Romans thought themselves far superior to the barbarians. He writes, "Only the God who is the God and Father of our Lord Jesus Christ has a heart big enough to hold all the world."

Remember: Jesus is The Real Thing! He came for everyone. He came to ease our doubt and despair. He came to take away our fear of death. Jesus is genuine.

Thought Pattern Interrupter: I can figure this out. Whatever is weighing on my mind this week, whatever has me baffled and not knowing which way to turn, I can figure it out with God's help.

Activity Suggestion: Call a nursing home and ask if you can donate something or volunteer your time. Perhaps there is a patient who never has a visitor. Perhaps there is something that you can do or donate that would brighten up the staff breakroom. Theirs isn't an easy job.

Comfort Recipe: Aunt Della's Chicken and Rice Casserole

This recipe from my Aunt Della brings back memories of the wonderful cook she was. Having a meal at her dining room table or kitchen table was a real treat.

- 2 cups chopped cooked chicken

- 1 cup diced celery

- 2 T. butter or margarine

- 2 cups cooked rice

- 14-oz can cream of chicken soup

- 1/2- to 3/4-cup mayonnaise

- 1 cup blanched almonds

Topping:
- 1 cup cornflakes, crumbled

- 2 T. melted butter or margarine

Preheat oven to 375 degrees F.

Saute celery and onion in 2 tablespoons of butter or margarine. Mix chicken, celery, onion, rice, soup, mayonnaise, and almonds together and pour into a greased 2-quart baking dish.

Bake for 45 minutes.

Meanwhile, melt 2 tablespoons butter or margarine. Stir crumbled cornflakes into the melted butter. Spread mixture on top of the casserole.

Return casserole to the oven and bake until slightly browned.

Yield: 4 to 6 servings, depending on appetites

The People Will See a Great Light

Setting the stage: The third chapter of Matthew is about the baptism of Jesus. The first 11 verses of the fourth chapter are about Jesus's time in the wilderness. Most Bible versions refer to these verses as the temptations of Jesus. In *The Gospel of Matthew, Vol 1, Revised Edition*, by William Barclay, the author says the Greek word in the original text was *peirazein*, which means tested. Tested has a different connotation than tempted.

Verses 12-14 of the fourth chapter of Matthew sweep us into a new chapter in the life of Jesus. He was, in effect, closing the door on his earlier life and stepping into the ministry chapter of his life. Verses 15 and 16 quote Isaiah 9:1-2. Those verses should sound familiar to you, for they were the scripture verses we looked at on Week 3.

When I picture the lands of the Bible, I tend to think of small, scattered villages with scant population; however, Barclay says that by moving to Capernaum, Jesus was moving into the densely populated district of Galilee. The district was 25 by 50 miles in area and contained more than three million people. There were 204 villages of at least 15,000 people each.

Matthew 4:12-17, as written in *The Message*: "When Jesus got word that John had been arrested, he returned to Galilee. He moved from his hometown, Nazareth, to the lakeside village Capernaum, nestled at the base of the Zebulun and Naphtali hills. This move completed Isaiah's revelation: Land of Zebulun, road to the sea, over Jordan, Galilee, crossroads for the nations. People sitting out their lives in the dark saw a huge light; Sitting in that dark, dark country of death, they watched the sun come up. This Isaiah-prophesied revelation came to life in Galilee the moment Jesus started preaching. He picked up where John left off: 'Change your life. God's kingdom is here.'"

Matthew 4:12-17, as written in *The Good News Bible*: "When Jesus heard that John had been put in prison, he went away to Galilee. He did not stay in Nazareth, but went to live in Capernaum, a town by Lake Galilee, in the territory of Zebulun and Naphtali. This was done to make come true what the prophet Isaiah had said, 'Land of Zebulun and land of Naphtali, on the road to the sea, on the other side of the Jordan, Galilee, land of the Gentiles! The people who live in darkness will see a great light. On those who live in the dark land of death the light will shine.' From that time Jesus began to preach his message: 'Turn away from your sins, because the Kingdom of heaven is near!'"

Matthew 4:12-17, as written in *The Living Bible*: "When Jesus heard that John had been arrested, he left Judea and returned home to Nazareth in Galilee; but soon he moved to Capernaum, beside the Lake of Galilee, close to Zebulun and Naphtali. This fulfilled Isaiah's prophecy: 'The land of Zebulun and the land of Naphtali, beside the Lake, and the countryside beyond the Jordan River, and Upper Galilee where so many foreigners live – there the people who sat in darkness have seen a great Light; they sat in the land of death, and the Light broke through upon them.' From then on, Jesus began to preach, 'Turn from sin, and turn to God, for the Kingdom of heaven is near.'"

Notice that Light is capitalized in verse 16.

Matthew 4:12-17, as written in *The New Oxford Annotated Bible (NRSV)*: "Now when Jesus heard that John had been arrested, he withdrew to Galilee. He left Nazareth and made his home in Capernaum by the sea, in the territory of Zebulun and Naphtali, so that what had been spoken through the prophet Isaiah might be fulfilled: 'Land of Zebulun, land of Naphtali, on the road by the sea, across the Jordan, Galilee of the Gentiles – the people who sat in darkness have seen a great light, and for those who sat in the region and shadow of death light has dawned.' From that time Jesus began to proclaim, 'Repent, for the kingdom of heaven has come near.'"

The footnote for verse 16 states, "The people who sat in darkness, those who suffered the most from the Assyrian invasions." The footnote for verse 17 is more involved: "From that time, the arrest of John (v. 12). The kingdom of heaven is Matthew's usual way of expressing the equivalent phrase, 'the kingdom of God,' found in parallel accounts in the other gospels. In asserting that God's kingdom has come near Jesus meant that all God's past dealings with his creation were coming to climax and fruition. Jesus taught both the present reality of God's rule (Luke 10.18; 11.20; 17.21) and its future realization (Matthew 6.10.)" [The only changes I made were to spell out books of the Bible where the original abbreviated them.] Notice that in this version of the Bible a chapter number and verse number are separated by a period instead of the traditional colon.

Matthew 4:12-17, as written in *TouchPoint Bible*: "When Jesus heard that John had been arrested, he left Judea and returned to Galilee. But instead of going to Nazareth, he went to Capernaum, beside the Sea of Galilee, in the region of Zebulun and Naphtali. This fulfilled Isaiah's prophecy: 'In the land of Zebulun and Naphtali, beside the sea, beyond the Jordan River – in Galilee where so many Gentiles live – the people who sat in darkness have seen a great light. And for those who lived in the land where death casts its shadow, a light has shined.' From then on, Jesus began to preach, 'Turn from your sins and turn to God, because the Kingdom of Heaven is near.'"

From *Matthew For Everyone Part 1*, by N.T. Wright, pages 27-28: "And in the case of Jesus, and of the way Matthew tells us about him, there is one thing supremely important: we need to know what this kingdom of heaven is that he said is approaching, and what action he expected people to take. Though this is central to everything Jesus was and did, and to everything that the gospels say about him, it is remarkable how few people really grasp what was going on."

Out of reverence to God, Matthew used "kingdom of heaven." Wright says, "Matthew wasn't referring to the place we go when we die; he was referring to the kingdom of God. Jesus knew the people He was talking to – 1st century Jews – would understand 'the kingdom of heaven....' This meant revolution."

Remember: In Matthew 4:12-14, Jesus stepped out of His comfort zone and into His time of ministry even as He knew how much trouble He would bring on Himself and how it would end. Not only was Jesus fully human, He was fully God. He knew and knows everything.

Thought Pattern Interrupter: God only made one me.

Activity Suggestion: Buy yourself a piece of jewelry or a new scarf to brighten up your winter wardrobe and lift your spirits.

See recipe for Slow Cooker Blackeyed Pea Stew on the next page.

Comfort Recipe: Slow Cooker Blackeyed Pea Stew

- 3 (15-oz.) cans blackeyed peas, undrained

- 1 large onion, finely chopped

- 2 medium-size carrots, peeled and chopped

- 1 (15-oz.) can diced tomatoes

- ½ teaspoon ground marjoram

- 2 bay leaves

- 1 cinnamon stick

- 1 (15-oz.) can whole-kernel corn, undrained

- ¼ teaspoon black pepper

- 1/8 teaspoon salt

Put all ingredients into a 3- or 4-quart slow cooker. Stir to mix. Cook on low for 6 or more hours. Discard bay leaves and cinnamon stick.

Freezes well in single- or two-serving portions.

Y'all Are the Light of the World

Scripture for this week: Matthew 5:13-16

Setting the stage: Did the title for this week's study get your attention? After reading pages 131-132 in *Reading the Bible with Rabbi Jesus: How a Jewish Perspective Can Transform Your Understanding*, by Lois Tverberg, I changed the title from "You are the light of the world" to "Y'all are the light of the world." Being a native North Carolinian, born of two native North Carolinians, saying "y'all" comes naturally to me.

It was enlightening for me to read what Lois Tverberg had to say about this in *Reading the Bible with Rabbi Jesus.* She explains that we should read the Bible as "we" instead of "you" because English speakers tend to take "you" as meaning them as individuals. In fact, she gives Matthew 5:14 as an example. English speakers tend to substitute their name for the word "you" in that verse. She maintains that Jesus was speaking to a group of people when he said "You are the light of the world." He went on to say, "A city on a hill cannot be hidden." A city is full of people; it's not an individual.

The English language limits our understanding because we don't have a word that distinguishes "you" as singular or plural. But, as Lois Tverberg points out, "American Southerners have an advantage here, because they use "y'all" when they address a group." Actually, y'all can be used when we address just two people, it doesn't have to be a group, but I'm nitpicking.

This gave me a new perspective and a new question. Jesus was addressing a group of people when he said, "You are the light of the world." But did He mean that the group was the light of the world or each individual believer is the light of the world? I tend to think he meant it both ways. If I think he meant that only Christians as a group are the light of the world, it lets me off the hook. It gives me a free pass. If I don't see myself as having an obligation or responsibility to be that light, I'll likely slack off and let others carry the load for me.

Dr. Tverberg, who is a Christian layperson, went on in the following pages to say we can still take Jesus' "you" personally. That's a relief, because as I studied Matthew 5:13-16 before reading Tverberg's book, I understood the passage to be directed at me as an individual. Her words are helpful, though, as a reminder that all together we are the body of Christ.

With that lengthy introduction, let's read the Scripture.

Matthew 5:13-16, as written in *The Message*: "Let me tell you why you are here. You're here to be salt-seasoning that brings out the God-flavors of this earth. If you lose your saltiness, how will people taste godliness? You've lost your usefulness and will end up in the garbage. Here's another way to put it: You're here to be light, bringing out the God-colors in the world. God is not a secret to be kept. We're going public with this, as public as a city on a hill. If I make you light-bearers, you don't think I'm going to hide you under a bucket, do you? I'm putting you on a light stand. Now that I've put you there on a hilltop, on a light stand – shine! Keep open house; be generous with your lives. By opening up to others, you'll prompt people to open up with God, this generous Father in heaven."

I love that imagery! God-colors. "You're here to be light" gives me purpose. It gives me an assignment – a job that is a privilege to do. But do I have the courage to do it?

Matthew 5:13-16, as written in *The Good News Bible*: "You are like salt for all mankind. But if salt loses its saltiness, there is no way to make it salty again. It has become worthless, so it is thrown out and people trample on it. You are like light for the whole world. A city built on a hill cannot be hid. No one lights a lamp and puts it under a bowl; instead he puts it on the lampstand, where it gives light for everyone in the house. In the same way your light must shine before people, so that they will see the good things you do and praise your Father in heaven."

Matthew 5:13-16, as written in *The Living Bible*: "You are the world's seasoning, to make it tolerable. If you lose your flavor, what will happen to the world? And you yourselves will be thrown out and trampled underfoot as worthless. You are the world's light -- a city on a hill, glowing in the night for all to see. Don't hide your light! Let it shine for all; let your good deeds glow for all to see, so that they will praise your heavenly Father."

Matthew 5:13-16, as written in *The New Oxford Annotated Bible (NRSV)*: "You are the salt of the earth; but if salt has lost its taste, how can its saltiness be restored? It is no longer good for anything, but is thrown out and trampled underfoot. You are the light of the world. A city built on a hill cannot be hid. No one after lighting a lamp puts it under a bushel basket, but on the lampstand, and it gives light to all in the house. In the same way, let your light shine before others, so that they may see your good works and give glory to your Father in heaven."

Matthew 5:13-16, as written in *TouchPoint Bible*: "You are the salt of the earth. But what good is salt if it has lost its flavor? Can you make it useful again? It will be thrown out and trampled underfoot as worthless. You are the light of the world – like a city on a mountain, glowing in the night for all to see. Don't hide your light under a basket! Instead, put it on a stand and let it shine for all. In the same way, let your good deeds shine out for all to see, so that everyone will praise your heavenly Father."

Let's see what William Barclay says about it.

***The Gospel of Matthew, Vol. 1*, by William Barclay, pages 122-126:** Barclay says "You are the light of the world" might just be "the greatest compliment that was ever paid to the individual Christian.... When Jesus commanded his followers to be the lights of the world, he demanded nothing less than that they should be like himself."

Barclay goes on to stress that we aren't expected to produce our own light. We are to reflect the radiance of Jesus Christ. He explains that in Jesus's time, once a lamp went out, it was hard to rekindle. He writes, "The primary duty of the light of the lamp was to be seen. So, then, Christianity is something which is meant to be seen." A person's Christianity should be evident in all their dealings in the world.

Barclay says that light is a guide. In that way, Christians are to make the way clear for other people. Once someone stands up against the crowd, others will follow their lead, but someone must go first. Christians should have the courage to go first.

It is sometimes the Christian's duty to be a warning – like a warning light, according to Barclay. He cautions us not to warn in anger, irritation, criticism, condemnation, and not in the desire to be hurtful. It needs to be out of love in order to be effective.

Barclay then explains that there are two different words for "good" in Greek. *Agathos* defines something as being good in quality. *Kalos*, he says, "means that a thing is not only good, but that it is also winsome and beautiful and attractive." The word used in this week's scripture passage is *kalos*.

"Winsome" is a word we don't hear often. It carries the connotation of a childlike charm.

With the distinction between *agathos* and *kalos* and the connotation of childlike charm in mind, you might want to stop here and go back to this week's Scripture. When you come across the word "good" in this week's Scripture, substitute the words "winsome, beautiful, and attractive."

The various versions of the Bible quoted in this week's devotional use the word "good" in the following ways: "the good things you do," "your good deeds," and "your good works." How often do we do our good deeds (like helping out with various church activities) out of a sense of obligation? Or perhaps we do volunteer work in the community. Do we do that activity with winsomeness, beauty, and attractiveness so others are led to thank and praise God for our deeds?

Barclay also emphasizes that our good deeds should not be done to draw attention to ourselves. They should be done to draw attention to God. In other words, instead of thinking about what we've done, Christians should think in terms of what God has enabled us to do. Barclay says as long as we think "of the praise, the thanks, the prestige... [we] have not really even begun on the Christian way."

I was editing this week's devotional a month into Donald J. Trump's second term as United States President. As a Christian, I was angry about how his administration was running roughshod over our democracy and attempting to make the biggest shift in the world order since the end of World War II. His attempt to align the US with Russia and put the US at odds with our northern neighbor, Canada, and with our historic European allies was frightening.

I wanted to lash out at Americans who still support Trump. Many of them professed to be Christians, but I could not understand how they continued to support a man who reflected none of the teachings of Jesus. I was angry at them for voting for him, and I was angry with him for what he was doing to our country and siding with Russia and against Ukraine in the midst of a war. After all, it was Russia that invaded the sovereign country of Ukraine.

The words of Barclay grabbed my attention! He was saying it was my duty as a Christian to be a warning, but he followed that by saying I needed not to warn in anger. That was a tall order! It prompted me to re-read this week's Scripture. Was Matthew 5:13-16 telling me to warn in love?

On October 7, 2023, Hamas and other militant groups from Gaza launched a terrorist attack on a music festival in Israel. They took 251 people hostage. Israel continued to bomb Gaza when this devotional book was published nearly two years later. As I did a "read aloud" proofread of this manuscript in mid-June 2025, the State of

Israel continued to restrict food and medical aid to Gaza. It amounted to a genocide by starvation at the hands of Israel's Prime Minister Benjamin Netanyahu, and yet the Trump Administration and many members of the U.S. Congress continued to support the nation of Israel.

As a Christian, is it my duty to speak out? If so, how do I do that out of love and not anger? How do I voice my opposition to the nation of Israel causing the children of Gaza to starve without coming across like I am anti-Semitic, when many Americans do not grasp the difference between people of the Jewish religion and the political entity of Israel? International university students in the United States were arrested and deported for taking part in pro-Gaza demonstrations. Freedom of speech and due process appeared to be ignored in many cases. How does a Christian speak out from a place of love and not a place of anger when he or she sees rights guaranteed in the U.S. Constitution being violated?

By the time you are reading this, that world crisis may have passed and been replaced by another crisis.

How can you respond or sound a warning out of love and not out of anger as a Christian when you see an injustice? How would Jesus respond? He is our example.

I re-read Matthew 5:13-16 in *The Message* and the thoughts I had written down after my initial reading as I wrote this devotional. I had an assignment as a Christian. It was and is to reflect God's love. That is a privilege, but it takes courage to carry that out — especially when my political views are at odds with those of some other Christians.

I re-read this week's Scripture in *The Good News Bible*. It reminded me that I am to reflect God's light in a way that will praise God.

William Barclay reminds me that it takes someone to be the first to stand up to a crowd and Christians should have the courage to be that person.

My mother taught me not to shrink in the face of opposition or a difficult situation. One of her favorite sayings was, "Stand on your own two feet."

I believe God is calling on me to stand on my own two feet. I just need to do that out of love and not anger.

Lashing out at people with a tone of condemnation is not going to prompt them to praise God. That is a lesson I am trying to learn as I write this book, as I respond to comments on my blog or other social media, and as I find my way in a chaotic world I no longer recognize.

I continue to seek God's will and guidance as I navigate this new world order. This is a difficult time to have a chronic illness.

Halley's Bible Handbook: "The greatest motive that a person can have is that, by his, or her, Manner of Life, others may be constrained to Glorify God."

That's a lot of responsibility! The various versions of Matthew 5:13-16, William Barclay's commentary, and Halley's Bible Handbook give us a lot to think about.

Remember: God is not a secret to be kept.

Thought Pattern Interrupter: I am a child of God.

Activity Suggestion: Donate to a homeless shelter.

Comfort Recipe: Easy No-Egg Cornbread

- 1 cup self-rising cornmeal mix

- 1 cup self-rising flour

- ¼ cup sugar

- ¼ cup vegetable oil

- 1 cup milk of your choice

- 2 teaspoons vinegar

- ½ cup cream-style corn

Put a 10-inch cast iron skillet in the oven. Heat oven (with the skillet in it) to 425 degrees.

Just before oven is preheated, mix all ingredients just until moistened.

Carefully remove cast iron skillet from the oven. Remember, it will be very hot, and it is heavy! Spray skillet with cooking spray and immediately pour batter into the hot skillet.

Bake for 25-30 minutes until golden brown. Remove from oven and carefully turn the cornbread out onto a round platter.

He is a Light to Reveal God to the Nations

Scripture for this week: Luke 2:32

Setting the stage: The context starts a few verses prior as we learn that Mary and Joseph had taken the baby Jesus to the temple to be circumcised. There was a good man named Simeon in Jerusalem. The Holy Spirit revealed to Simeon that he would see the Messiah before he died.

Led by the Holy Spirit, he went into the temple. Simeon took Jesus in his arms and told God He could take him (Simeon) now because the promise had been fulfilled. He said, "With my own eyes I've seen your salvation; it's now out in the open for everyone to see: A God-revealing light to the non-Jewish nations, and of glory for your people Israel."

This verse is part of Simeon's proclamation to those in the temple that this baby – this Jesus – was sent from God to enlighten the world about the Heavenly Father.

On page 146 of *Reading the Bible with Rabbi Jesus: How a Jewish Perspective Can Transform Your Understanding*, by Lois Tverberg, the author says that "Israel" in this passage is referring to the Family of Abraham. Those of us who were born after the establishment of the present-day country known as Israel, sometimes have trouble remembering that.

The Israel in the Bible is the Family of Abraham. The political State of Israel was formed by the United Nations in 1948. Keep in mind as you read the Bible that references to Israel are to the Jewish people and not the modern-day political state of Israel.

Luke 2:32 is a message to Jews and Gentiles (everyone who is not a Jew.) In other words, Simeon was proclaiming that the Christ child was the Messiah for all people. Jesus was a Jew. In Luke 2:32, Simeon was proclaiming that Jesus was the bridge between Gentiles and Jews.

Luke 2:32, as written in *The Message*: "A God-revealing light to the non-Jewish nations, and of glory for your people Israel."

Luke 2:32, as written in *The Good News Bible*: "A light to reveal your will to the Gentiles and bring glory to your people Israel."

Luke 2:32, as written in *The Living Bible*: "He is the Light that will shine upon the nations, and he will be the glory of your people Israel."

Luke 2:32, as written in *The New Oxford Annotated Bible* *(NRSV)*: "a light for revelation to the Gentiles and for glory to your people Israel."

Luke 2:32, as written in *TouchPoint Bible*: "He is a light to reveal God to the nations, and he is the glory of your people Israel."

My thoughts: Look at the phrases in the various versions: "God-revealing light," "A light to reveal your [God's] will," "he is the Light," "a light for revelation," and "He is a light to reveal God."

Each of the five versions of the Bible in this devotional uses the word "light" or "Light." That tells me that the concept of Jesus being the Light is of utmost importance. The focus will be on Jesus and the Light that shines from and through Him will show the way for all people. The verse goes on to include the Gentiles.

That doesn't surprise Christians today. Of course Jesus came to be a light – The Light – for us! But step back and put yourself in the place of the Jews hearing Simeon speak those words in the temple in Jerusalem. Jerusalem – of all places! Simeon is proclaiming that this baby Jesus is the Messiah. The men hearing this were expecting a Jewish king – not a baby who had come for Jews and non-Jews. They must have thought Simeon had lost his mind.

I can just imagine some of the things they said behind Simeon's back... "He's old. You know how confused old people can get." And perhaps they didn't just say that behind his back. We aren't privy to the discussions that took place that day or the days thereafter.

Moving through to the next phrase in the verse, we see that Simeon also included the Jews. "...for glory to your people Israel;" "and bring glory to your people Israel;" "and he will be the glory of your people Israel;" and "he is the glory of your people Israel."

Simeon understood the potential of Jesus, even if he didn't know that the Jewish authorities would eventually reject Jesus. Little did he know what would happen some thirty years in the future.

Remember: Jesus came to light my way

Thought Pattern Interrupter: I will find something good in each day, even if it's winter and I'm cold and cannot get warm.

Activity Suggestion: Visit a friend in person, if possible, or on the phone if you cannot get out and about.

Comfort Recipe: Marie's Cereal Mix

My sister took a recipe and adapted it to be healthier than a typical cereal mix. Cereal snack mixes are usually baked and contain butter or other fats. Marie's recipe is simple and quick to make.

- 4 cups Cinnamon Chex cereal

- 1 cup chopped pecan pieces

- 1 cup small pretzel squares or mini-pretzels

- ½ cup dark chocolate chips

In a large bowl, mix all ingredients. Place in airtight container(s). Yield: About 20 one-half-cup servings

Notes: Cinnamon Chex Cereal is half sweet cinnamon squares and half rice Chex cereal. At Christmas, consider substituting a cup of red and green M&M candies for the chocolate chips.

Your Body Fills with Light

cripture for this week: Matthew 6:22-23

Setting the stage: This passage talks about eyes. There is a lot of imagery in these two verses, especially in *The Message*. But before we get into this week's Scripture selection, I will share some related things I learned from Lois Tverberg's book, *Walking in the Dust of Rabbi Jesus: How the Jewish Words of Jesus Can Change Your Life*. She devotes an entire chapter of her book to "Gaining a Good Eye."

Tverberg writes, "The Hebrew language uses 'eye' in many idioms that describe a person's attitude toward others.... Having a 'good eye' (*ayintovah*) is to look out for the needs of others and be generous in giving to the poor. But to have a 'bad eye' (*ayin ra'ah*) is to be greedy and self-centered, blind to the need of those around you." In this way, the Hebrew language includes attitude and response toward others in the understanding of the concept of "seeing."

Tverberg says not understanding Jesus' use of such figures of speech regarding the "eye," will lead us to misinterpret some of His teachings. She says in the parlance of the Jews, "your 'eye' is really about your attitude toward money." Jesus wants His followers to be generous with their monetary resources.

In that same chapter, Tverberg writes that "... our relationship with money reveals our relationship with God." Also, "... if you're radically convinced of God's caring presence in your life, you're also confident that God will provide for your needs – not just materially, but emotionally and spiritually as well. You may not be wealthy by the world's standards, but you have a rock-solid understanding that what you have is enough,...."

"Good eye" or "bad eye" in the Bible gets to the nitty-gritty of what motivates you in your life. Keeping Tverberg's words about the Hebrew meaning of "good eye" and "bad eye" illuminate Matthew 6:22-23 and other passages in the Bible. I found her explanations enlightening.

Matthew 6:22-23, as written in *The Message*: "'Your eyes are windows into your body. If you open your eyes wide in wonder and belief, your body fills up with light. If you live squinty-eyed in greed and distrust, your body is a musty cellar. If you pull the blinds on your windows, what a dark life you will have!'"

I love this passage in *The Message*! Squinty-eyed! We all know what that means. The words give us a great visual of what greed looks like.

We all know what musty smells like. "Musty cellar" gives us an image of an undesirable environment. In fact, when we read those words, we may even recall a time and place where we smelled something musty. For a second, the actual smell becomes palpable.

The "eyes as windows into your body" is an image we've all heard – or more specifically, I've heard that the eyes are a window into the soul.

There's so much imagery in these two verses, they could serve as a teaching tool in a writing class.

Matthew 6:22-23, as written in *The Good News Bible*: "The eyes are like a lamp for the body. If your eyes are sound, your whole body will be full of light; but if your eyes are no good, your body will be in darkness. So if the light in you is darkness, how terribly dark it will be!"

Here, we change perspective as the eyes are lamps instead of windows. It brings to my mind that when I was a child in the 1950s in North Carolina, I knew some people who called window panes "window lights." It never made sense to me, but maybe there's a connection.

Matthew 6:22-23, as written in *The Living Bible*: "If your eye is pure, there will be sunshine in your soul. But if your eye is clouded with evil thoughts and desires, you are in deep spiritual darkness. And oh, how deep that darkness can be!"

The Living Bible's paraphrased version of the Bible is a darker version than the one in *The Message*, but this is a serious matter. It's not about the difference between light and dark. It's about the difference between The Light (Jesus Christ) and the Dark (being separated from Jesus Christ.)

I'm eager to see what the other two versions have to say, so let's keep reading.

Matthew 6:22-23, as written in *The New Oxford Annotated Bible (NRSV)*: "The eye is the lamp of the body. So, if your eye is healthy, your whole body will be full of light; but if your eye is unhealthy, your whole body will be full of darkness. If then the light in you is darkness, how great is the darkness!'"

This version introduces the idea of health as it compares the light a healthy eye lets in with the darkness an unhealthy eye lets in.

Cataracts are growing in both my eyes. To replicate what I can see and not see when I'm driving at night and facing oncoming vehicle headlights, my ophthalmologist shines a bright light in my eyes one at a time and asks me to read the eye chart. This might not be a good analogy to verses 22 and 23 because with my cataracts it comes down to degrees of obstructed sight, whereas with Jesus Christ you either believe in Him or you don't. There's no gray area.

Matthew 6:22-23, as written in *TouchPoint Bible*: "Your eye is a lamp for your body. A pure eye lets sunshine into your soul. But an evil eye shuts out the light and plunges you into darkness. If the light you think you have is really darkness, how deep that darkness will be!"

This version surprised me. It introduces an evil eye. The term "evil eye" is a belief or superstition that one can cast a curse on another person by glaring at them. It's usually preceded by the word "the." But this definition of "evil eye" didn't seem to fit verses 22 and 23.

I began searching on the internet for other explanations. One source said when found in the Bible "evil eye" does not refer to a curse-causing stare, but is used to describe a stingy person. It speaks to a person's outlook on life, their personality, their attitude.

The *Touch Point Bible* gives us the contrast of a pure eye and an evil eye. Re-read this Scripture in the *Touch Point Bible*, substituting "a stingy attitude" for "an evil eye."

Let's see what William Barclay has to say about these verses.

The Gospel of Matthew, Volume 1, Revised Edition, by William Barclay, pages 243-247: The heading William Barclay gives these two verses is "The Distorted Vision." He explains it as "the spiritual state of the eye through which it [light] has to pass, for the eye is the window of the whole body."

Barclay then gives examples of things that can distort our spiritual vision. Prejudice heads the list. Jealousy can cloud our judgment. Self-conceit is the other trait on Barclay's list. Self-conceit trips us up two ways: It prevents us from seeing ourselves as we really are and from seeing others as they really are.

Barclay also goes back to the original Greek manuscript. I always appreciate it when a pastor is able and takes the time to do that. It almost always gives valuable clues to the meaning of a Bible passage.

Barclay points out that eye is written in the singular in this passage. He says in the Greek language "the word for single is *haplous*, and its corresponding noun is *haplotēs*. Regularly in the Greek of the Bible these words mean generous and generosity."

Now the "stingy" reference in the *Touch Point Bible* is making more sense.

Barclay goes on to address the word "evil." The Greek manuscript used the word *ponēros*. He says *ponēros* "regularly means... grudging" in the New Testament and in the Septuagint. (The Septuagint is a Greek version of the Hebrew Bible, or Old Testament, made for Greek-speaking Jews in Egypt in the third and second centuries BC.) He goes on to say it can translate as ungenerous. Barclay concludes that in verses 22 and 23 Jesus is saying, "'There is nothing like generosity for giving you a clear and undistorted view of life and of people; and there is nothing like the grudging and ungenerous spirit for distorting your view of life and of people.'"

Let that sink in. There is a deep truth in that statement.

Barclay recommends that we be generous in judging others as well as generous in our actions. He states that feeling the pain of others as if it is our own pain will lead us to "begin to see people and things clearly. It is then that our eye becomes full of light."

Barclay closes his comments about Matthew 6:22-23 with these words: "The grudging eye distorts our vision: the generous eye alone sees clearly, for it alone sees as God sees."

My thoughts: Matthew 6:22-23 is one of the shortest Scripture passages highlighted in this devotional book, so I find it interesting that I ended up with one of the longest chapters for it. Of all the passages examined in this book, I think there were more differences in key words used across the five versions of the Bible for these two verses than in any other Scripture in this book.

We've looked at light, lamp, window, eye, pure, evil, greed, distrust, squinty-eyed, musty cellar, sound eyes, eyes that are no good, healthy eye, unhealthy eye, sunshine into the soul, plunges into darkness, prejudice, jealousy, and self-conceit.

It all comes down to the fact that we need The Light – Jesus Christ.

The writer in me couldn't help but notice that every version of the Bible I looked at ended verse 23 with an exclamation point. I wondered how many exclamation points are in the Bible. It varies from version to version, but they are rare. Exclamation points are supposed to be used sparingly, and the Bible appears to be a good example. Hebrew and Greek don't use punctuation, so it's not a carryover from the original manuscripts.

Remember: I need the light, but even more, I need The Light – Jesus Christ.

Thought Pattern Interrupter: I'll make a point to see the good in others.

Activity Suggestion: Call a local Ronald McDonald House or other such facility and ask what they need. A batch of cookies? Paper products? Toiletries? Pre-packaged snack food? Children's books? Stuffed animals?

See the recipe for Presbyterian Hospital Chili on the next page.

Comfort Recipe: Presbyterian Hospital Chili

They didn't serve this at the old Presbyterian Hospital on Hawthorne Lane in Charlotte, but one of the employees submitted it for inclusion in a fundraiser cookbook. Buying that cookbook was perhaps the best thing that came out of my hospital stay in the early 1980s. I made several adjustments to the list of ingredients and amount to suit my taste. (For instance, I omit the half-pound of bacon to make it less expensive and healthier.) I've made this chili every fall and winter since 1993. I hope you enjoy it as much as I have.

- ½ pound bacon, cut in small cubes (optional)

- 1 small onion, chopped

- ½ green bell pepper, chopped

- 6 celery ribs, chopped

- 2 pounds ground beef

- Salt and pepper to taste

- 2 teaspoons chili powder (optional)

- 1 (15-oz.) can tomato sauce

- 1 (6-oz.) can tomato paste

- 1 tomato sauce can of water

- 1 small tomato paste can of water

- 3 (15-oz.) cans dark red kidney beans, drained and rinsed

In a large skillet or stock pot, fry bacon (if using), until brown. Drain on paper towels. Add onion, bell pepper, celery, and ground beef. Break up ground beef and fry until there is no pink in the beef. Drain off excess grease. Add salt, pepper, and chili powder to taste. Add tomato sauce and paste and one can each of water. Add beans and simmer for several hours. Stir occasionally to prevent sticking. You can add more water if that becomes a problem.

Freezes well. Yield: Lots!

No One Lights a Lamp then Hides It

Setting the stage: This verse immediately brings to my mind the occasions when the power goes out. Being without electricity in the 21st century can abruptly throw us into a panic. We take electric lights for granted. We even turn them on when we don't need them.

Luke 8:16, as written in *The Message*: ("Misers of What You Hear" is the heading for Luke 8:16-18 in *The Message*.) "No one lights a lamp and then covers it with a washtub or shoves it under the bed. No, you set it up on a lamp stand so those who enter the room can see their way."

I stopped reading, but curiosity got the best of me. Why was the heading "Misers of What You Hear"? I kept reading and in verses 17 and 18 I found an explanation of verse 16. In other words, verses 17 and 18 shine a light on verse 16.

Luke 8:17-18 in *The Message*: "We're not hiding things; we're bringing everything out into the open. So be careful that you don't become misers of what you hear. Generosity begets generosity. Stringiness impoverishes."

This made me want to know what came before verse 16. It was the parable of the sower. Luke 8:11 says the seed is the Word of God. You'll remember in the parable Jesus compares our hearing the Word of God with seeds that fall in various places. Sometimes they take root but soon wither. Sometimes they just fall by the wayside, get trampled, and never get a chance to grow.

This was the context in which Jesus talks about putting a lamp on a lampstand instead of hiding it – and He comes full circle in verses 17-18 in which he refers to people hearing the Word of God (seeing the light/Light) but keeping it to themselves.

Verses 17-18 are a warning to the audience Jesus had that day, but they are just as much a warning to us today.

Let's look at some other versions of the Bible, reading all three verses.

Luke 8:16-18, as written in *The Good News Bible*: "No one lights a lamp and covers it with a bowl or puts it under a bed. Instead, he puts it on the lampstand, so that people will see the light as they come in. Whatever is hidden away will be brought out into the open, and whatever is covered up will be found and brought to light. Be careful, then, how you listen; because whoever has something will be given more, but whoever has nothing will have taken away from him even the little he thinks he has."

Luke 8:16-18, as written in *The Living Bible*: "[Another time he asked, 'Who ever heard of someone lighting a lamp and then covering it up to keep it from shining? No, lamps are mounted in the open where they can be seen. This illustrates the fact that someday everything [in men's hearts] shall be brought to light and made plain to all. So be careful how you listen; for whoever has, to him shall be given more; and whoever does not have, even what he thinks he has shall be taken away from him.'"

Luke 8:16-18, as written in *The New Oxford Annotated Bible (NRSV)*: "'No one after lighting a lamp hides it under a jar, or puts it under a bed, but puts it on a lampstand, so that those who enter may see the light. For nothing is hidden that will not be disclosed, nor is anything secret that will not become known and come to light. Then pay attention to how you listen; for to those who have, more will be given; and from those who do not have, even what they seem to have will be taken away.'"

Luke 8:16-18, as written in *TouchPoint Bible*: "'No one would light a lamp and then cover it up or put it under a bed. No, lamps are mounted in the open where they can be seen by those entering the house. For everything that is hidden or secret will eventually be brought to light and made plain to all. So be sure to pay attention to what you hear. To those who are open to my teaching, more understanding will be given. But to those who are not listening, even what they think they have will be taken away from them.'"

That version helped me. I was having trouble getting the meaning of that last sentence!

The Gospel of Luke, Revised Edition, **by William Barclay, pages 100-102:** About verse 16, William Barclay says, "The Christian, however humble his position and his sphere, must never be ashamed to show his colours."

Barclay continues, "Verse 16 stresses the essential conspicuousness of the Christian life. Christianity is in its very nature something which must be seen. It is easy to find prudential reasons why we should not flaunt our Christianity in the world's face. In almost every person there is an instinctive fear of being different. The world is always likely to persecute those who don't conform to pattern."

About verse 17, Barclay writes, "There's folly in trying to hide something from ourselves. The truth will eventually come out if we try to hide things from others. Trying to hide something from God is impossible."

And the essence of what Barclay says about verse 18 is that if you stay fit, you can do more. The flabbier you get, the more you lose ability to do. "This is just another way of saying that there is no standing still in life. All the time we are either going forward or going back. The seeker will always find; but the man who stops seeking will lose even what he has."

My thoughts: What's the first thing we do when the power goes off? At my house, we grope around until we locate a flashlight or an emergency battery-powered light.

What do we do with that battery-powered light? We don't hide it. We don't put it under a bed. We put it on a table so all in the room can see it and, more importantly, all in the room can see to get around without stumbling into furniture or falling down.

The next thing we do is call Duke Energy to report the power outage and try to ascertain how long the power will be out.

What William Barclay says about verse 18 struck a chord with me and helped me to see an analogy for the verse in my own experience. I took piano lessons in elementary school, but I didn't practice and didn't develop the talent I had. In junior high, I played the flute in the school band, but I didn't practice or stick with it. Today, I probably couldn't get a pleasant sound out of a flute. In later life, I've tried to learn how to play the dulcimer. I love the instrument, but I do not practice on a regular basis. When I take my dulcimer out of its case, I feel like I'm starting over like the first time I picked it up.

If you don't flex your Bible study muscles, they'll become flabby and you'll lose the understanding you thought you had.

My examination of Luke 8:16 took me on an unexpected journey. I started by taking a literal look at a lamp that should be placed in a high place instead of hidden away, but then the Scripture took me into the deeper meaning of Jesus's teachings and a warning about paying attention to those teachings and being open to a better understanding. Verses 16 through 18 should get our attention.

Remember: Remember to let your light shine!

Thought Pattern Interrupter: It's a sign of strength to ask for help.

Activity Suggestion: Invite a neighbor for coffee or tea (or hot chocolate!)

Comfort Recipe: Savory Ham and Rice

- 4 cups cooked brown rice (or white rice, if you prefer)

- 2 tablespoons margarine

- ¼ cup chopped onion

- ½ pound ham cut into 2-inch strips or 1/2-inch square chunks

- 1 teaspoon salt

- 2 tablespoons brown sugar

Cook rice according to package directions or use 4 cups leftover rice. Melt margarine in skillet; add onion and ham and sauté. Add cooked rice and remaining ingredients. Stir gently until hot. Freezes well.

Yield: 4-6 servings

It Bears Repeating, No One Lights a Lamp then Hides It

Setting the stage: Part of this Scripture passage will sound familiar to you because it's very much like Luke 8:16-18, which we looked at last week. I considered combining both passages for last week, but there are nuances in Luke 11:33-36 that prompted me to separate them for two weeks as I originally planned.

Luke was a physician, so he included or emphasized some things that the other three Gospels omitted or paid less attention to.

Every version of this passage that I read and its almost identical passages in other books of the Gospel use the term "lamp stand." Even *The Message*, which is in our contemporary vernacular uses the term. But what did a 1st century A.D. lamp stand look like?

I went to my tablet and searched for "1st century lamp stand" online. I had to sift through the images of lamps from the 1960s to find several examples of "Roman bronze lamp with stand." They appeared to be two to three feet tall and three-legged. They had some style to them and the elongated lamps sitting atop them were more ornate than I expected, with fancy handles curving up at one end.

Hang in there with me and let's see what today's four verses tell us.

Luke 11:33-36, as written in *The Message*: "No one lights a lamp, then hides it in a drawer. It's put on a lamp stand so those entering the room have light to see where they're going. Your eye is a lamp, lighting up your whole body. If you live wide-eyed in wonder and belief, your body fills up with light. If you live squinty-eyed in greed and distrust, your body is a musty cellar. Keep your eyes open, your lamp burning, so you don't get musty and murky. Keep your life as well-lighted as your best-lighted room."

Luke 11:33-36, as written in *The Good News Bible*: "No one lights a lamp and then hides it or puts it under a bowl; instead, he puts it on the lampstand, so that people may see the light as they come in. Your eyes are like a lamp for your body. When your eyes are sound, your whole body is full of light; but when your eyes are no good, your whole body will be in darkness. Make certain, then, that the light in you is not darkness. If your whole body is full of light, with no part of it in darkness, it will be bright all over, as when a lamp shines on you with its brightness."

The part that jumped out at me was, "Make certain, then, that the light in you is not darkness." We learned in Week 9 that darkness is separation from Jesus Christ.

Luke 11:33-36, as written in *The Living Bible*: "No one lights a lamp and hides it! Instead, he puts it on a lampstand to give light to all who enter the room. Your eyes light up your inward being. A pure eye lets sunshine into your soul. A lustful eye shuts out the light and plunges you into darkness. So watch out that the sunshine isn't blotted out. If you are filled with light within, with no dark corners, then your face will be radiant too, as though a floodlight is beamed upon you."

"Lustful eye" jumped out at me. How did we get from "squinty-eyed in greed and distrust" in *The Message*, to "Lustful eye" in *The Living Bible*? "Squinty-eyed" has a much different connotation than "lustful." Let's keep going and see if we can connect all the dots.

As written in *The New Oxford Annotated Bible (NRSV)*: "No one after lighting a lamp puts it in a cellar, but on the lampstand so that those who enter may see the light. Your eye is the lamp of your body. If your eye is healthy, your whole body is full of light, but if it is not healthy, your body is full of darkness. Therefore consider whether the light in you is not darkness. If then your whole body is full of light, with no part of it in darkness, it will be as full of light as when a lamp gives you light with its rays."

Some of the wording sounds odd and isn't clear, such as "The light in you is not darkness." It's easier to discern what something is than what it is not.

Luke 11:33-36, as written in *TouchPoint Bible*: This version is similar in wording for verses 33-34a, so let's start with verse 34.

"Your eye is a lamp for your body. A pure eye lets sunshine into your soul. But an evil eye shuts out the light and plunges you into darkness. Make sure that the light you think you have is not really darkness. If you are filled with light, with no dark corners, then your whole life will be radiant, as though a floodlight is shining on you."

The more I read, the less clear this passage became. "Evil eye" jumps out at me. We learned in Week 9 that "evil eye" means a stingy person or stingy attitude, a lack of generosity. Does it mean an evil way of looking at the world or other people?

We read "squinty-eyed" in *The Message*, "eyes are no good" in *The Good News Bible*, "lustful eye" in *The Living Bible*, "eye that's not healthy" in *The New Oxford Annotated Bible (NRSV)*, and "evil eye" in the *Touch Point Bible*.

I'm eager to see what renowned Minister of the Gospel in the Church of Scotland, William Barclay had to say about Luke 11:33-36.

The Gospel of Luke, Revised Edition, **by William Barclay, pages 152-154:** Barclay's title for his interpretation of Luke 11:33-36 caught my attention. He called this passage "The Darkened Heart." I thought that was an interesting synonym for the "live squinty-eyed" phrase in *The Message*.

I was relieved to read that Barclay said this could be a difficult passage to grasp. He wrote, "... the light of life depends on the heart" just as "the light of the body depends on the eye." He went on to write, "If the heart is right the whole life is irradiated with light; if the heart is wrong all life is darkened. Jesus urges us to see that the inner lamp is always burning. What then is it that darkens the inner light? What is it that can go wrong with our hearts?"

He goes on to expand on these three ways in which something can go wrong with our hearts: They can become hard (as in falling into a habit of doing something that in the beginning we knew was wrong); they can become dull (as in getting so used to hearing a Scripture over and over again that we stop really listening); and they can become actively rebellious (as in ignoring how God is trying to guide us even when we know we should do what He is telling us to do).

Barclay has a talent for giving illustrations that get right to the point – or right to the heart – of a verse's meaning. I must share with you a story he tells to illustrate how our hearts can become dull. Here it is quoted in its entirety:

"Florence Barclay tells how when she was a little girl she was taken to church for the first time. It was Good Friday, and the long story of the crucifixion was read and beautifully read. She heard Peter deny and Judas betray; she heard Pilate's bullying cross-examination; she saw the crown of thorns, the buffeting of the soldiers; she heard of Jesus being delivered to be crucified, and then there came the words with their terrible finality, 'and there they crucified Him.' No one in the church seemed to care; but suddenly the little girl's face was buried in her mother's coat, and she was sobbing her heart out, and her little voice rang through the silent church, 'Why did they do it? Why did they do it?' That is how we should feel about the Cross, but we have heard the story so often that we can listen to it with no reaction at all. God keep us from the heart which has lost the power to feel the agony of the Cross – borne for us."

Remember: Indeed! How is it that we can read or hear the passages about the Crucifixion of Christ and not react?

Thought Pattern Interrupter: Jesus died for my sins, so I need to let His Light shine through my face and my actions even when the daylight hours are short and I feel sad about the season.

Activity Suggestion: Make a list of everything you're thankful for.

Comfort Recipe: Mexican One Dish

If you like a dish with a Mexican flare that you can make without dirtying several pots and pans, you'll like this easy main dish that's made in just one skillet. Just pair it with a salad for a complete meal.

- 1 pound ground beef

- 2 tablespoons or as much as one envelope of taco seasoning, to taste

- ¾-cup beef broth

- 1 (15-oz.) can diced tomatoes

- ½ cup salsa

- 2 cups frozen corn, thawed

- 2½ cups sharp cheddar cheese, divided

In a large skillet brown the ground beef. Drain any grease. Add taco seasoning, beef broth, tomatoes, salsa, and corn. Heat through. Add 2 cups of cheese and heat through for about 10 minutes or until cheese is melted. Add ½ cup cheese on top. Can be topped with corn chips or tortilla chips.

Yield: 4 servings

Parable of the Lost Coin

Scripture for this week: Luke 15:8-10

Setting the stage: In *Halley's Bible Handbook*, Henry H. Halley describes the fifteenth chapter of Luke as "the calm after the storm" in Luke 14. In the fourteenth chapter of Luke, Jesus doesn't beat around the bush as He talks about the price people will pay for following Him. He goes on to explain that He must be first in our lives. We must love Him more than we love anyone else. It's enough to make a person question the wisdom of following Jesus!

But then we come to Luke 15. It is a beautiful chapter about the tender, forgiving grace of Jesus. The chapter includes the Parable of the Lost Sheep, the Parable of the Prodigal Son, and the passage we're looking at this week: The Parable of the Lost Coin.

Luke 15:8-10, as written in *The Message*: "Or imagine a woman who has ten coins and loses one. Won't she light a lamp and scour the house, looking in every nook and cranny until she finds it? And when she finds it you can be sure she'll call her friends and neighbors: 'Celebrate with me! I found my lost coin!' Count on it – that's the kind of party God's angels throw every time one lost soul turns to God."

At first glance, we might be tempted to think, What's the big deal? It's just a coin! But let's keep reading and see what that coin must have meant to the woman in the parable.

Luke 15:8-10, as written in *The Good News Bible*: "Or suppose a woman who has ten silver coins loses one of them – what does she do? She lights a lamp, sweeps her house, and looks carefully everywhere until she finds it. When she finds it, she calls her friends and neighbors together, and says to them, 'I am so happy I found the coin I lost. Let us celebrate!' In the same way, I tell you, the angels of God rejoice over one sinner who repents."

Luke 15:8-10, Luke 15:8, as written in *The Living Bible*: "Or take another illustration: A woman has ten valuable silver coins and loses one. Won't she light a lamp and look in every corner of the house and sweep every nook and cranny until she finds it? And then won't she call in her friends and neighbors to rejoice with her? In the same way there is joy in the presence of the angels of God when one sinner repents."

Luke 15:8-10, as written in *The New Oxford Annotated Bible (NRSV)*: "'Or what woman having ten silver coins, if she loses one of them, does not light a lamp, sweep the house, and search carefully until she finds it? When she has found it, she calls together her friends and neighbors, saying, "Rejoice with me, for I have found the coin that I had lost." Just so, I tell you, there is joy in the presence of the angels of God over one sinner who repents.'"

There is a footnote on page 106 of *The New Oxford Annotated Bible (NRSV)* that gives added perspective about this passage. It states, "This parable intensifies the picture of human helplessness and divine concern. The coin was approximately equivalent to the denarius."

According to sources I've checked, a denarius was equal to a day's wage. Most of us would be frantic if we misplaced that much money.

Another way to look at it is to take it literally. It says the woman only had ten coins. She didn't have money in the bank. She didn't have investments or a 401K Plan where she worked. The woman apparently only had ten coins, so when she lost one of them, she lost ten percent of her money. It's easy in the 21st century to belittle her loss: one measly coin. Put yourself in her place. Regardless of how much money you have in your wallet, in the bank, and in various investments, what if one day you realized you'd lost ten percent of all of it?

That puts the story in a new light!

Luke 15:8-10, as written in *TouchPoint Bible*: "Or suppose a woman has ten valuable silver coins and loses one. Won't she light a lamp and look in every corner of the house and sweep every nook and cranny until she finds it? And when she finds it, she will call in her friends and neighbors to rejoice with her because she has found her lost coin. In the same way, there is joy in the presence of God's angels when even one sinner repents."

***The Gospel of Luke, Revised Edition*, by William Barclay, pages 209-210:** Barclay explains how difficult it would have been to find a lost coin in a Palestinian peasant's house. He describes the typical house of that time and place as being very dark. The only source of natural light would have been a circular window approximately 18 inches in diameter. Barclay says dried reeds and rushes would have covered the dirt floor of the house.

Barclay offers two possible reasons the woman so desperately searched for her coin and why she was ecstatic when she found it: (1) It was equal to a day's pay for a man in Palestine; and (2) A married woman in Palestine at that time would have worn a head-dress "made of ten silver coins linked together by a silver chain." Barclay compares the loss of one of those coins to a woman today losing her wedding ring.

Isn't it wonderful to know that our loving God seeks us even more intensely than the woman searched for her lost coin? That is the point of the story. Barclay says this concept of God was beyond the imagination of the Jews hearing this story for the first time.

We are the coin in this parable. We are sinners, and God looks for us. He is always ready to welcome us with open arms. Imagine His joy when one of us who has turned our back on Him eventually comes around, repents, and accepts His forgiveness!

My thoughts: Let's look at it another way and try to zero in on the real lesson this parable is meant to teach us.

Suppose you get paid every two weeks. Suppose there are no banks and no direct deposit. You're paid in cash. On your way home from work, something happens. Perhaps you're robbed. Or maybe you're in an accident, left unconscious. When you wake up, your money is gone.

That would be a terrible thing. Hours later, though, someone calls you to say they found your wallet and will bring it to you. Your first thought might be, *It's probably empty. All today's pay is probably gone.* Imagine your joy when you get the wallet back and count the money.

It's all there! It's time to celebrate! Celebrate just like the angels do when a sinner repents.

That's the heart of the parable, but why does each version of verse 8 make a point to mention light? Every version I've read states or asks about the woman lighting a lamp to search the house for the lost coin.

Is that not why God sent Jesus Christ to us? Christ serves as our light and our lamp when we are lost or when we're at our wit's end. Christ is the Light that will help us find our way when we're lost. He is the Light that will come to our rescue when we've lost all hope and don't know which way to turn. He is eagerly waiting for us to turn to Him – just as verse 10 tells us that God's angels are overjoyed when one of us acknowledges our mistakes or shortcomings, tells God we're sorry, and strives to sin no more.

Remember: God is always eager to forgive you.

Thought Pattern Interrupter: I'm doing the best I can, and that's all I can do.

Activity Suggestion: Write a letter to someone you don't want to lose touch with or someone you need to apologize to.

See recipe for Spoonburgers on the next page.

Comfort Recipe: Spoonburgers

You might call these sloppy joes, but my mother called them spoonburgers. I have a hunch she got the recipe off a can of Campbell's Chicken Gumbo Soup. I remember them from my early childhood and I still enjoy the recipe today. It always brings fond memories of my mother to mind.

She always made spoonburgers in a cast iron skillet but, now that I have a ceramic cooktop, I can't use her skillet except in the oven.

- 1 pound ground beef

- 1 small onion, chopped

- 1 teaspoon salt

- Sprinkle of black pepper, or to taste

- 1 teaspoon mustard

- 1 tablespoon Worcestershire sauce

- 1/3 cup ketchup

- 1 (15-oz.) can chicken gumbo soup

- Buns, or this is good served over rice

Brown the meat and chopped onion. Drain off any grease. Add the other ingredients and mix. When mixture starts to cook, turn the temperature down to low. Stir occasionally to prevent sticking. Simmer until thick enough to spoon onto buns, or serve over rice.

Yield: about 6-8 servings

The Word was the Source of Life and This Life Brought Light to Mankind

Setting the stage: Let's go back to the beginning of The Gospel According to John in *The Good News Bible*. "Before the world was created, the Word already existed; he was with God, and he was the same as God. From the very beginning the Word was with God. Through him God made all things; not one thing in all creation was made without him."

"The Word" in this passage is Jesus.

The introduction to The Gospel According to John in *The Good News Bible* opens with these words: "The Gospel of John presents

Jesus as the eternal Word of God, who 'became a human being and lived among us.'"

Without that explanation, the opening verses of John can be confusing. He speaks of the Word being a "he," but to someone new to Christianity, it might not be clear that "the Word" is Jesus.

The introduction to The Gospel According to John in *The New Oxford Annotated Bible (NRSV)* explains that Jesus was with God from the beginning and participated with God in creating everything.

The introductory remarks about the Gospel of John in the *Touch Point Bible* reminds us that the author of John set out to describe or explain the divinity of Jesus. Whereas Matthew and Luke give us Jesus's human lineage, John wants those of us who didn't see Jesus when He walked on the earth in human form to know that Jesus existed with God from the beginning. That introduction states, "John's purpose was not to write another biography of Jesus' life on earth but to reveal Jesus as God's Son and even as God himself."

With that established, let's look at five versions of John 1:4.

John 1:4, as written in *The Message*: "What came into existence was Life, and the Life was Light to live by."

John 1:4, as written in *The Good News Bible*: "The Word was the source of life, and this life brought light to mankind."

John 1:4, as written in *The Living Bible*: "Eternal life is in him, and this life gives light to all mankind."

John 1:4, as written in *The New Oxford Annotated Bible (NRSV)*: "What has come into being in him was life, and the life was the light of all people." (*The New Oxford Annotated Bible (NRSV)* splits this sentence, with "What has come into being" shown as the last part of verse 3 and the rest of the sentence given as verse 4.)

John 1:4, as written in *TouchPoint Bible*: "Life itself was in him, and this life gives light to everyone."

***Halley's Bible Handbook*, by Henry H. Halley says this about John 1:4 on page 429:** "Jesus the Light of the World," reminds us that Jesus referred to himself as the Light of the World numerous times throughout the New Testament. Halley goes on to say, "It means that Jesus, as the Light of the World, is the One who makes clear the Meaning and Destiny of Human Existence."

***The Gospel of John, Vol I, Revised Edition*, by William Barclay, pages 42-46:** William Barclay dedicated five pages to John 1:4. My initial reaction to that was, *Who am I to attempt to write about John 1:4, if it took a theologian five pages of fine print to explain it?*

Barclay's writings are very organized. He delineates each point he thinks is important. He starts his comments on verse 4 by quoting numerous verses in the New Testament where Jesus talked about life. He says that the Gospel of John contains the word life more than 35 times, and the verb to live or to have life more than 15 times.

With that, Barclay asks what John means by life. He lists (with more detailed explanation) that (1) John means life is the "opposite of destruction, condemnation and death." (2) That although Jesus is "the bringer of this life," God is the source and the giver. (3) "When Jesus came offering men eternal life, He was inviting men to enter into the very life of God." (I've read his paragraph about eternal life several times, and I must admit I don't fully understand what he's saying; therefore, I'll just leave it at that. (4) We enter that life by believing in

Jesus Christ. (By that, Barclay says we "must be convinced that Jesus is really and truly the Son of God.")

Also, there has to be more than an intellectual belief. Barclay states, "To believe in Jesus means to take Jesus at his word, to accept his commandments as absolutely binding, to believe without question that what he says is true."

Barkley continues, "For John, belief means the conviction of the mind that Jesus is the Son of God, the trust of the heart that everything that Jesus says is true and the basing of every action on the unshakable assurance that we must take him at his word. When we do that we stop existing and begin living. We know what Life with a capital L, really means."

Then, Barclay addresses the word Light. John uses the word 21 times. "Jesus, as John says here, is the light of men." John the Baptist's purpose was to point people to the Light.

To Barclay, three things stand out about Jesus' Light. (1) "The light which Jesus brings is the light which puts chaos to flight." He refers to the first verses of Genesis. (2) "The light which Jesus brings is a revealing light. It is the condemnation of men that they loved the darkness rather than the light; and they did so because their deeds were evil; and they hated the light lest their deeds should be reproved. The light which Jesus brings is something which shows things as they are." (3) "The light which Jesus brings is a guiding light." Barclay concludes his comments about John 1:4 with, "Without Jesus we are like men groping on an unknown road in a black-out. With Him the way is clear."

Remember: Jesus Christ always has been, is, and always will be.

Thought Pattern Interrupter: I am good enough.

Activity Suggestion: Call your local animal shelter and ask if you can volunteer to walk the dogs or even read to them!

Comfort Recipe: Aunt Lila Mae's Chocolate Pie

- 1 cup sugar

- 3 tablespoons flour

- 3 tablespoons cocoa

- 1/8 teaspoon salt

- 2 eggs

- 4 tablespoons margarine, melted

- ½ teaspoon vanilla

- 1 cup milk

- 1 unbaked pie shell, 8- or 9-inch

Mix together the sugar, flour, cocoa, and salt. Add the eggs, melted margarine, and vanilla. Mix well and gradually add the milk. Stir until smooth. Pour into unbaked 8- or 9-inch pie shell. Bake 10 minutes at 425 degrees. Reduce heat to 350 degrees and continue baking until center seems firm.

A note about Aunt Lila Mae: Aunt Lila Mae was the closest thing I ever had to a grandmother, since both my grandmothers died before I was born. Aunt Lila Mae was my mother's only sister who survived to adulthood. She was a very quiet, unassuming person, but she took great pride in her chocolate pies.

After she moved into a senior residential center and no longer did any cooking or baking, my mother would invite her for a meal occasionally and always made a chocolate pie by Aunt Lila Mae's recipe. It got to be a family joke that Aunt Lila Mae would taste my mother's pie and always say, "It's almost as good as mine!"

When my mother wrote down the recipe for me when I first got out on my own as a young adult, she added the following note: "If you bake many chocolate pies some day you may bake one 'almost as good' as Aunt Lila Mae's."

The Life-Light Blazed Out of the Darkness; the Darkness Couldn't Put it Out

Scripture for this week: John 1:5

Setting the stage: This verse follows John 1:1-4, which we studied last week. Remember our examination of John 1:4? Re-read that verse – or better yet, read from the first verse in John's first chapter to get your bearings.

Those earlier verses mention the Word, Life, and Light – all capitalized, and then in verse 5 as written in The Message, John gives us a new hyphenated word for Jesus Christ: Life-Light.

Let's see how five versions of the Bible present verse 5.

John 1:5, as written in The Message: "The Life-Light blazed out of the darkness; the darkness couldn't put it out."

John 1:5, as written in *The Good News Bible*: "The light shines in the darkness, and the darkness has never put it out."

John 1:5, as written in *The Living Bible*: "His life is the light that shines through the darkness – and the darkness can never extinguish it."

John 1:5, as written in *The New Oxford Annotated Bible (NRSV)*: "Darkness is total evil in conflict with God; it cannot overcome."

John 1:5, as written in TouchPoint Bible: "The light shines through the darkness, and the darkness can never extinguish it."

My thoughts: Those are five only slightly different images and wording.

(1) *The Message* gives us a new moniker for Christ: "Life-Light." What imagery *The Message* gives us! The verse opens with "The Life-Light blazes out of the darkness." *Merriam-Webster's Collegiate Dictionary, Tenth Edition*, 2001, defines the verb blaze as follows: "to burn brightly; to flare up; to be conspicuously brilliant or resplendent; to shoot rapidly and repeatedly; or to proceed extremely rapidly." I think the "to be conspicuously brilliant or resplendent" suits this verse – suits this Life-Light. You may have a different take on that.

(2) *The Good News Bible* presents the image in two different tenses: "The light shines [present tense] in the darkness, and the darkness has never [present perfect tense] put it out." I couldn't figure out

what tense "has never" was without looking it up. The explanations surprised me. They said that the word "never" has nothing to do with the verb it's connected to. I had to refresh my memory about present perfect tense. (I never was good at the names of tenses of speech once I got beyond past and present.) Without burdening you or me with an English teacher's definition, I think for our purposes we just need to think of the second part of verse 5 like this: "Has never put it out" means action which began in the past and continues into the present.

(3) *The Living Bible* uses present tense and goes a step further when it ends the verse with the words "darkness can never extinguish it." I like that. It drives home the fact – the promise and the assurance – that the forces of evil will never defeat Jesus Christ.

(4) *The New Oxford Annotated Bible (NRSV)* uses fewer words to translate verse 5, but it doesn't comfort me like *The Living Bible's* words.

(5) *TouchPoint Bible*'s wording is similar to that of *The Living Bible*.

Let's look at a couple of Bible commentaries and see if we can grasp a deeper meaning of John 1:5.

***The Gospel of John, Vol. I, Revised Edition*, by William Barclay**. To John there was a darkness in the world that was as real as the light. On page 47, Barclay writes, "Sinning man loves the darkness and hates the light, because the light shows up too many things." Barclay goes on to say, "So John is saying: 'Into this world there comes Jesus, the light of the world; there is a darkness which would seek to eliminate him [Jesus], to banish him from life, to extinguish him. But there is a power in Jesus that is undefeatable. The darkness can hate him, but it can never get rid of him.'"

Barclay sees life without Christ as a life spent in darkness. He thinks it is important to look at the Greek word *Katalambanein* which has been translated as "put out" or "extinguished" in today's versions of the Bible. He explains that there are three meanings to the word in Greek: "(1) It could mean that the darkness never understood the light.... A man cannot understand Christ until he first submits to Christ. (b).... *Katalambanein* can mean to pursue until one overtakes and so lays hold on and overcomes." This could mean that the darkness of the world had done everything possible to eliminate Jesus Christ, even to crucifying Him, but it could never destroy Him.... (c) It can be used as extinguishing a fire or flame. That is the sense in which we have taken it here. Although men did all they could to obscure and extinguish the light of God in Christ, they could not quelch it. In every generation the light of Christ still shines in spite of the efforts of men to extinguish the flame."

The Layman's Bible Commentary, Vol. 19: John. This commentary addresses verse 5 on page 30 as follows: "Here a dark note enters the picture: the darkness in verse 5 is more than absence of light; it is an active rejection of God's will, a hostile darkness that opposes the working of the divine Light."

My mother often taught an adult women's Sunday School class or the Bible lesson at a Women of the Church circle meeting. This was one of her books. She had underlined this sentence on page 31: "This Light did more than shine (verse 5). He enlightened the spirit, mind, and heart of every man."

Remember: Jesus Christ shines through the darkness but the darkness fails to contain Him. The forces working against Him when He walked on the earth in human form failed to contain Him. Even when they nailed Him to the cross and He died a temporary death, they still couldn't get rid of Him. They still haven't. They never will!

Thought Pattern Interrupter: Nothing can happen today or this week that God and I together can't handle.

Activity Suggestion: Sit down with a cup of Beth's Hot Chocolate (recipe below) and with each sip name something or someone you're thankful for.

Comfort Recipe: Beth's Hot Chocolate

My niece, Beth, made this wonderful slow cooker hot chocolate years ago when we visited her in Georgia for Christmas. It's the best hot chocolate I've ever had!

- 1½ cups heavy cream

- 1 (14-oz.) can sweetened condensed milk

- 6 cups milk

- 1 teaspoon vanilla

- 2 cups semi-sweet chocolate chips

In a slow cooker, stir together heavy cream, sweetened condensed milk, milk, vanilla, and chocolate chips. Cover and cook on LOW for 2 hours, stirring occasionally, until mixture is hot and chocolate chips are melted. Stir again before serving. Top with your favorite fixings and enjoy!

Refrigerate any leftovers.

Yield: 12 cups

People Working and Living in Truth Welcome God-Light

Scripture for this week: John 3:19-21

Setting the stage: To get the whole picture, it's good to read John 3:1-21 for this conversation Jesus had with Nicodemus, a respected Jewish teacher. The Scriptures say that Nicodemus went to Jesus at night. Don't miss that point. Nicodemus admits that God sent Jesus to teach "us" and that only one sent by God could perform the miracles Jesus had performed. But as a respected Jewish teacher, Nicodemus needed some answers.

In verse 3, Jesus responds that He came as more than a teacher. He tells Nicodemus he must be "born again" if he has any chance of seeing the Kingdom of God. Nicodemus takes Jesus literally and argues that he cannot enter his mother's womb and be born again. In verses 10-21,

Jesus explains what he meant by "born again." Jesus explains that a person has to be baptized with water and the Holy Spirit. That's what He meant in verse 4 when He told Nicodemus he must be born again. In his explanation, Jesus foretells of His crucifixion in verse 14 and His coming back to life after His crucifixion in verse 15. And, of course, there's John 3:16-17 in which Jesus proclaims the saving love of God and that God sent Him (Jesus) to save the world, not to condemn the world. Verses 18-21 tell us that we condemn ourselves if we turn our backs on God and reject Jesus. But if we choose to follow Jesus, we live unafraid in His Light.

In the third chapter of John, Jesus is trying to explain to Nicodemus that a person has to be baptized with water and the Holy Spirit. That's what Jesus meant in John 3:4 when he told Nicodemus he must be born again.

John 3:19-21, as written in *The Message*: "This is the crisis we're in: God-light streamed into the world, but men and women everywhere ran for the darkness. They went for darkness because they were not really interested in pleasing God. Everyone who makes a practice of doing evil, addicted to denial and illusion, hates God-light and won't come near it, fearing a painful exposure. But anyone working and living in truth and reality welcomes God-light so the work can be seen for the God-work it is."

Verse 21 begins with, "But...." When a sentence begins with "But...," you definitely need to read what came before. God-light streamed into the world, but men and women everywhere chose to remain in the dark because they wanted to keep sinning and thought they could just turn their backs on the love God offered them through Jesus Christ. They weren't interested in pleasing God.

Reread verse 21 above. The wording in *The Message* is somewhat vague for me, but maybe that's just me. For one thing, I get hung up on the word "truth." When *The Message* was published in 2002, there was general agreement about the definition of the word; however, in the 2020s that word has been hijacked by the political arena in the United States and its meaning has become twisted. We aren't so sure what the truth is anymore. But, we can be sure of the truth proclaimed by Jesus Christ.

John 3:19-21, as written in *The Good News Bible*: "This is how the judgment works: the light has come into the world, but people love the darkness rather than the light, because their deeds are evil. Anyone who does evil things hates the light and will not come to the light, because he does not want his evil deeds to be shown up. But whoever does what is true comes to the light in order that the light may show that what he did was in obedience to God."

The Good News Bible version is actually a little easier for me to understand than *The Message* version this time. If you do what you think is right in the eyes of God, you aren't afraid of God. You're not afraid for His Light to shine on you. You're not afraid for God's Light to shine through you so others can see it.

Isn't that our assignment from Jesus Christ? For me, this points to Jesus Christ's new Commandment: "Love the Lord your God with all your heart and love others as you love yourself." If we follow that commandment, John 3:19-21 will be covered. If you strive to obey Jesus' new Commandment, you don't have to worry about a ton of do's and don'ts. Isn't that freeing?

Jesus came to make life easier for us. He came to uncomplicate all the rules and regulations of The Old Testament. Jesus said, "Love the Lord your God with all your heart and love others as you love yourself." I'm not implying that commandment is easy to accomplish. Far from it!

But if we strive to live that commandment, we will strive not to put other gods before God, we will strive not to make or worship an idol, we will strive not to take the name of God in vain, we will strive to set aside the Sabbath as a holy day, we will strive to honor our parents, we will not murder anyone, we will strive not to commit adultery, we will strive not to steal, we will strive not to tell a lie, and we'll strive not to wish we had what someone else has. Do those things sound familiar? They're the Ten Commandments, but aren't they all covered by the new commandment Jesus gave us?

It's difficult to live within those commandments. I dare say, it's impossible. We aren't perfect. God doesn't expect us to be perfect. He expects us to try. And when we mess up – God is always just a prayer away and eager to forgive us. That's amazing grace!

What does that have to do with John 3:19-21? In an effort to get to the crux of the passage, I went down that rabbit hole, but I felt led to do so. Forgive me if I've led you astray, but I don't think it's a huge leap from John 3:19-21 to Jesus' new commandment. Let's look at three other versions of the Bible and see what they say.

John 3:19-21, as written in *The Living Bible*: "Their sentence is based on this fact: that the Light from heaven came into the world, but they loved the darkness more than the Light, for their deeds were evil. They hated the heavenly Light because they wanted to sin in the darkness. They stayed away from that Light for fear their sins would be exposed and they would be punished. But those doing right come gladly to the Light to let everyone see that they are doing what God wants them to."

"Their sentence" at the beginning of verse 19 seems like unusual wording until we read the preceding verses. John 3:18 says, "There is no eternal doom awaiting those who trust him to save them. But those who don't trust him have already been tried and condemned for not believing in the only Son of God."

The Living Bible capitalizes Light and presents the passage in past tense – both of which give a different perspective than *The Message* or *The Good News Bible*. I think *The Message* and *The Good News Bible* grab my attention more than *The Living Bible* in this case because they come across as a warning to me in my daily life. *The Living Bible*, by being in past tense, sounds like its talking about people back in Biblical times and not about me.

John 3:19-21, as written in *The New Oxford Annotated Bible (NRSV)*: In reading this version, let's go back to verse 16. John 3:16 is a Bible verse with which many people are familiar. In reading John 3:16-21, in the following paragraph, notice the quotation marks. These are Jesus' words to Nicodemus, a Pharisee and Jewish leader who recognized Jesus as a teacher sent by God. Nicodemus was a member of the Sanhedrin. The quotation marks in this version serve to remind us that these are the words of Jesus in answer to Nicodemus when Nicodemus was having trouble understanding what it meant "to be born again."

"'For God so loved the world that he gave his only Son, so that everyone who believes in him may not perish but have eternal life. Indeed, God did not send the Son into the world to condemn the world, but in order that the world might be saved through him. Those who believe in him are not condemned; but those who do not believe are condemned already, because they have not believed in the name of the only Son of God. And this is the judgment, that the light has come

into the world, and people loved darkness rather than light because
their deeds were evil. They hated the heavenly Light because they
wanted to sin in the darkness. They stayed away from that Light for
fear their sins would be exposed and they would be punished. But
those who do what is true come to the light, so that it may be clearly
seen that their deeds have been done in God.'"

The footnote for John 3:16 in *The New Oxford Annotated Bible
(NRSV)* is, "Luther called this verse 'the Gospel in miniature.' The
footnote for verses 17-20 says, "God's purpose is to save; individuals
judge themselves by hiding their evil deeds from the light of Christ's
holiness."

John 3:19-21, as written in *TouchPoint Bible*: Verse 19 in
Touch Point Bible is almost identical to that verse in *The Living Bible*
and *The New Oxford Annotated Bible*. Verses 10-21 in the third chapter of John are printed in red to remind us that they are the words of
Jesus. Verses 19-21 read as follows: "'Their judgment is based on this
fact: The light from heaven came into the world, but they loved the
darkness more than the light, for their actions were evil. They hate the
light because they want to sin in the darkness. They stay away from
the light for fear their sins will be exposed and they will be punished.
But those who do what is right come to the light gladly, so everyone
can see that they are doing what God wants.'"

I wish I'd read these verses in *TouchPoint Bible* first! It spells it out
in simpler terms than the other versions.

Let's see what Rev. William Barclay said in *The Gospel of John, Vol
1, Revised Edition*.

The Gospel of John, Vol 1, Revised Edition, **by William Barclay, pages 138-140:** Barclay addresses John 3:17-21 under the subtitle, "Love and Judgment."

Barclay points out the paradox of the love Jesus speaks about in John 3:16 and the judgment he talks about in John 3:19. Barclay sheds some light here. He says if a person is confronted with Jesus but rejects Jesus, he has condemned himself. Jesus offers nothing but love; it is the human being who condemns himself, not Jesus. A person's reaction to Jesus lays his soul bare, according to Barclay.

Barclay clarifies some things in John 3:19-21 for me, but I find his take on the verses overall to be a downer.

The Layman's Bible Commentary, Vol. 19: This commentary states, "Only by that Spirit-caused renewal can man enter the Kingdom of God."

My thoughts: By referring to God's presence as light and His absence as darkness, John illustrates in terms those of us with eyesight and access to light and to darkness can understand. Light and dark are opposites in the same way that accepting Jesus Christ as your Lord and Savior and rejecting Him are opposites.

The light in John 3:19 is the presence of God and the darkness is God's absence where a person rejects God's love through Jesus Christ. God chooses us, but He gives us the gift of free will. It's our choice. Do we choose to walk in the light – the presence – of Jesus or do we choose darkness? Is that not the crux of the Gospel?

Barclay emphases the doom of the person who rejects Jesus. I prefer the more positive approach I surmise from verse 21. If you live right, you'll be all right in God's eyes. I'm not a proponent of "the feel good gospel" some TV evangelists proclaim, but I do prefer to concentrate on the love and forgiveness of God rather than the "hell fire and damnation" some believers dwell on out of fear.

In the beginning, I studied verses 19-21 individually. I think that was helpful, but they really need to also be studied together.

Remember: The Light is Jesus Christ. When we are in the Light, there is no pretense.

Thought Pattern Interrupter: I will find something to laugh about today.

Activity Suggestion: Write a letter to your younger self.

Comfort Recipe: Black Bean Soup

- 1 onion, chopped

- 3 (15-oz.) cans black beans

- 6 cups chicken broth

- 2 teaspoons salt

- 3 cups cooked rice or 1 box Long Grain & Wild Rice, cooked by package instructions

- Grated cheese, for garnish

- Tortilla chips, crushed, for garnish

- Sour cream, for garnish

In a large saucepan, saute chopped onion in a small amount of olive oil until onions are translucent. Add black beans, chicken broth, and salt. Cook on medium heat until nice and hot. (You don't need to bring it to a boil.)

Divide the cooked rice between six soup bowls. Spoon the soup over the rice. Top with the other toppings.

Yield: 6 servings

The Light of the World

S cripture for this week: John 8:12

Setting the stage: Jesus was talking to people in the Temple. Religion scholars and Pharisees had just brought in a woman caught in adultery. (Begs the question: Where was the man who was caught in adultery with her, but we all know the man wasn't thought to be guilty of sinning. The more things change, the more they stay the same, but I digress.)

Jesus shamed the scholars and Pharisees into leaving after asking who among them was sinless. Then, Jesus told the woman He didn't condemn her and told her to go and sin no more.

That brings us to verse 12.

John 8:12, as written in *The Message*: "Jesus once again addressed them: 'I am the world's Light. No one who follows me stumbles around in the darkness. I provide plenty of light to live in.'"

Such statements about Himself infuriated the Jewish leaders.

Note: In *Reading the Bible with Rabbi Jesus: How a Jewish Perspective Can Transform Your Understanding*, Lois Tverberg states on page 261: "Paraphrases such as *The Message* are also not useful for word study because they render the original language so loosely." I, however, continue to use *The Message* because its late-20th century vernacular is easier to understand than some other versions.

John 8:12, as written in *The Good News Bible*: "Jesus spoke to the Pharisees again, 'I am the light of the world,' he said. 'Whoever follows me will have the light of life and will never walk in darkness.'"

John 8:12, as written in *The Living Bible*: "Later, in one of his talks, Jesus said to the people, 'I am the Light of the world. So if you follow me, you won't be stumbling through the darkness, for living light will flood your path.'"

John 8:12, as written in *The New Oxford Annotated Bible* (NRSV): "Again Jesus spoke to them, saying, 'I am the light of the world. Whoever follows me will never walk in darkness but will have the light of life.'"

The footnote for John 8:12-59 states, "Great golden lamps in the temple court were lit during the Festival of Booths (7:2): therefore the appropriateness of Jesus' claims in v. 12 (Isa 49:6; 60:1-3)...."

The Festival of Booths/Feast of Booths/Feast of Tabernacles/Sukkot is a seven-day harvest holiday celebrated in the Jewish month Tishrei, four days after Yom Kippur. It is one of three religious holidays during which Jews are required to go to temple, so there would have been a great number of people at the temple on this occasion.

John 8:12, as written in *TouchPoint Bible*: "Jesus said to the people, 'I am the light of the world. If you follow me, you won't be stumbling through the darkness, because you will have the light that leads to life.'" (In this verse Jesus is referring to Isaiah 9:1-2. In Week 3, we talked about Isaiah's prophecy about the coming of Jesus Christ as a baby.)

***The Gospel of John, Vol 1, Revised Edition*, by William Barclay, pages 10-11:** Barclay says the argument Jesus had with the Jewish authorities in verse 12 was in the Temple Treasury. It would have been a busy place as people came to place their offerings in one or more of the thirteen treasure chests against a wall. Each chest was designated for a specific offering. (Barclay goes into detail about the various offerings, but that information is not germane to the point or significance of the verse.)

Barclay explains that "the evening of the first day [of the Festival of Booths/Feast of Booths/Feast of Tabernacles/Sukkot] there was a ceremony called The Illumination of the Temple." In the center of the Court of Women there would have been four great candelabra that lit up every courtyard in Jerusalem when they were lighted."

It was, therefore, no coincidence that Jesus chose this time and place to proclaim, "I am the world's Light" (*The Message*), and "I am the light of the World." (*NRSV*).

To grasp the effect Jesus' claim would have had on the scribes and Pharisees, it helps to look at how His audience used the word light. As Jews, they associated the word light with God. Barclay states, "The Rabbis declared that the name of the Messiah was Light." Since they didn't think Jesus was the Messiah, they saw it as blasphemous that He would claim to be the Light of the World.

Without two witnesses to testify to Jesus being the Light of the World, the Jewish officials could not accept what Jesus said. They required evidence.

Knowing that the Rabbis would have taken Jesus' saying that He was the Light of the world as blasphemous adds a layer of understanding and a dangerousness to this week's Scripture.

My thoughts: I still like *The Message* as a resource because in some cases it presents Scripture in terms I can understand when some other versions of the Bible are not clear to me. I will keep Lois Tverberg's comment in mind, though, as I continue to use *The Message* as a supplemental Bible resource. Knowing about The Illumination of the Temple ceremony helps put Jesus' announcement that he was the light of the world in perspective. He always gave examples and illustrations that would have been understandable to His audience.

Remember: Jesus lights your path.

Thought Pattern Interrupter: God is my constant companion.

Activity Suggestion: Call a friend or relative.

Comfort Recipe: Slow Cooker Chicken Chili
- 1 pound boneless, skinless chicken breasts

- 1 onion, diced

- 1 clove garlic, minced (or 2, if you prefer)

- 3 cups chicken broth

- 2 (15-oz.) cans great northern beans, drained and rinsed

- 1 (15-oz.) can whole kernel corn, drained

- 1 teaspoon salt

- A sprinkle of ground black pepper

- ½ teaspoon cumin

- ¾ teaspoon oregano

- 4 ounces cream cheese, softened and cut into cubes

Combine all ingredients except the cream cheese in slow cooker. Let cook on low for 8 hours. Just before serving, remove chicken breasts to a cutting board. Shred the chicken and return it to the slow cooker. Stir in the cream cheese cubes, cover, and cook on high for 15 more minutes.

Note: If you want to decrease the cooking time. Substitute cooked and already shredded chicken.

Those Who Walk in the Dark Don't Know Where They're Going

Scripture for this week: John 12:35-36

Setting the stage: Jesus' public ministry was drawing to a close. Six days before Passover, Jesus went to visit His friends, Lazarus, Martha, and Mary. In John 12:3 Mary anointed Jesus' feet with expensive perfume and was chastised by Judas Iscariot for not selling the perfume and giving the money to the poor. But Jesus came to Mary's defense. He told Judas Iscariot that the perfume was for His (Jesus') burial. In verse 8 Jesus said, "You always have the poor with you, but you do not always have me." He was trying to prepare His friends and disciples for His crucifixion, which was fast approaching.

The chief priests were angry because so many Jews had started following Jesus after he raised Lazarus from the dead. They planned to kill Lazarus because they blamed him for the increase in people deserting Judaism to follow Jesus. A great crowd gathered as word spread that Jesus was coming to Jerusalem. Even some Greeks had come and requested to meet Jesus. No wonder the Jewish authorities were nervous. Jesus was becoming too popular. As Jesus approached Jerusalem, His followers took branches from palm trees and greeted Him as he came riding a young donkey. Christians celebrate that occasion still today as Palm Sunday.

Jesus tried to explain to His listeners that day that he would soon be lifted up to heaven. They were confused by this because they had been taught that the Messiah would be here forever. It was this exchange that led up to Jesus' reply in John 12:35-36.

Let's look at those two verses in five versions of the Bible.

John 12:35-36, as written in *The Message*: "Jesus said, 'For a brief time still, the light is among you. Walk by the light you have so darkness doesn't destroy you. If you walk in darkness, you don't know where you're going. As you have the light, believe in the light. Then the light will be within you, and shining through your lives. You'll be children of light.'"

John 12:35-36, as written in *The Good News Bible*: "Jesus answered, 'The light will be among you a little longer. Continue on your way while you have the light, so that the darkness will not come upon you for the one who walks in the dark does not know where he is going. Believe in the light, then, while you have it, so that you will be the people of the light.'"

John 12:35-36, as written in *The Living Bible*: "Jesus replied, 'My light will shine out for you just a little longer. Walk in it while you can, and go where you want to go before the darkness falls, for then it will be too late for you to find your way. Make use of the Light while there is still time; then you will become light bearers.'"

The footnote for "light bearers": Literally, "sons of light." I like "light bearers" and the explanatory footnote, "sons of light." I'd prefer "children of light," of course, but *The Living Bible* was published in 1971 before people started using more inclusive language. If I am a child of the light, I take that to mean the DNA of the light/The Light is in essence in my DNA. Am I going too far? I don't know the answer to that, so I just offer it for you to think about.

John 12:35-36, as written in *The New Oxford Annotated Bible (NRSV)*: "Jesus said to them, 'The light is with you for a little longer. Walk while you have the light, so that the darkness may not overtake you. If you walk in the darkness, you do not know where you are going. While you have the light, believe in the light, so that you may become children of light.'"

John 12:35-36, as written in *TouchPoint Bible*: "Jesus replied, 'My light will shine out for you just a little while longer. Walk in it while you can, so you will not stumble when the darkness falls. If you walk in the darkness, you cannot see where you are going. Believe in the light while there is still time; then you will become children of the light.'"

***The Gospel of John, Vol 1, Revised Edition*, by William Barclay, pages 130-137:** Barclay's take on these verses is that they give us a promise and a threat. The promise is the light we walk in if we accept Jesus. The threat is that at some point it will be too late for us to decide to trust in and accept Jesus.

In this passage, Jesus was urging His listeners to accept Him before His crucifixion, or it would be too late. Barclay says the eternal truth here is, "In Christ the supreme blessedness is offered to men; in one sense it is never too late to grasp it; but nonetheless it remains true that it must be grasped in time."

Remember: Even if you're old and think it's too late for you to accept Jesus, it's not too late.

Thought Pattern Interrupter: I will find something beautiful today.

Activity Suggestion: Make muffins or cornbread to share with a neighbor or friend.

Comfort Recipe: Creamy Cornbread

- 1 cup self-rising flour

- ½ cup vegetable oil

- 2 eggs

- 1 (8-oz.) can cream-style corn

- 1 (8-oz.) container sour cream

Mix all ingredients well. Pour into a buttered 9-inch pie plate.
Bake at 350 degrees for 40 minutes.
Freezes well.

I Came as a Light so No One Who Believes in Me Should Stay in Darkness

Scripture for this week: John 12:46

Setting the stage: Beginning in John 12:44, Jesus is saying if you believe in Him, you believe in God the Father who sent Him. And in the verses that follow John 12:46, Jesus says He did not come to judge, but those who reject Him will be judged by the words that He has spoken.

John 12:46, as written in *The Message*: "I am Light that has come into the world so that all who believe in me won't have to stay any longer in the dark."

John 12:46, as written in *The Good News Bible*: "I have come into the world as light, so that everyone who believes in me should not remain in darkness."

John 12:46, as written in *The Living Bible*: "I have come as a Light to shine in the dark world, so that all who put their trust in me will no longer wander in the darkness."

John 12:46, as written in *The New Oxford Annotated Bible (NRSV)*: "I have come as light into the world, so that everyone who believes in me should not remain in the darkness."

John 12:56, as written in *TouchPoint Bible*: "I have come as a light to shine in the dark world, so that all who put their trust in me will no longer remain in the darkness."

***The Gospel of John, Vol 2, Revised Edition*, by William Barclay, page 135:** According to Barclay, John said verses 44-50 in the 12th chapter of John's Gospel "are Jesus's last words of public teaching." After these words, Jesus taught His disciples. In this larger passage, Jesus states that He came to save the world, not to condemn the world.

My thoughts: It was out of love that God sent Jesus to walk in the world in human form. Jesus came as a light – The Light – to a dark world. All a person has to do to live forever in God's glorious heaven is to accept Jesus as their Lord and Savior. That's all! Accept Jesus and live in the Light of Christ. Let His Light shine through you and all around you. You'll never have to be afraid of the Dark again because the Light and Saving Grace of God the Father, Jesus the Son, and the Holy Spirit abide in you.

Remember: Accept Jesus and live fearlessly in the Light of Christ.

Thought Pattern Interrupter: Every snowflake is unique, and so am I.

Activity Suggestion: Send a "Thinking of you" card or note to someone who lives alone.

See recipes for Brunswick Stew on the next page.

Comfort Recipe: Brunswick Stew

- 1½ pounds skinless, boneless chicken breasts, cut into pieces about 1/2-inch square

- 3 medium potatoes, cut into pieces about 1/2-inch square

- 1 medium carrot, chopped (about ½ cup)

- 1 (28-oz.) can crushed tomatoes, undrained

- 1 (15-oz.) can lima beans, drained

- 2 (15-oz.) cans cream-style corn

- 1 tablespoon Worcestershire sauce

- ¾ teaspoon salt

- ½ teaspoon dried marjoram leaves

- 8 slices bacon, cooked and crumbled

Mix all ingredients except bacon in 3½- to 6-quart slow cooker. Cover and cook on low heat setting 8 to 10 hours (or high for 3 to 4 hours) or until potatoes are tender. Stir in crumbled cooked bacon.

Freezes well.

Paul on the Road to Damascus

Scripture for this week: Acts 9:1-9

Setting the stage: Read Acts 9:1-25 and Acts 22:1-10 to get the whole picture.

Saul was a Pharisee. He was a Roman citizen, which carried with it certain privileges. He set out to destroy the Christian church. He was on his way to Damacus to ferret out the Christians there when he was struck blind. It was a life-changing event of such magnitude that he converted to Christianity and his name was changed to Paul.

The first two verses of Acts 9 in *The Message* give a concise and easily understood build up to the passage we're looking at this week: "All this time Saul was breathing down the necks of the Master's disciples, out for the kill. He went to the chief Priest and got arrest warrants to take to the meeting places in Damascus so that if he found anyone there belonging to the Way, whether men or women, he could arrest them and bring them to Jerusalem."

"The Way" is found several times in The Book of Acts (or The Acts of the Apostles) to refer to the followers of Jesus. The origin of their referring to themselves as followers of The Way probably comes from Jesus referring to himself as "the way, and the truth, and the life" in the Gospel of John 14:6.

Acts 9:3-9, as written in *The Message*: "He set off. When he got to the outskirts of Damascus, he was suddenly dazed by a blinding flash of light. As he fell to the ground, he heard a voice: 'Saul, Saul, why are you out to get me?' He said, 'Who are you, Master?' "I am Jesus, the One you're hunting down. I want you to get up and enter the city. In the city you'll be told what to do next.' His companions stood there dumbstruck – they could hear the sound, but couldn't see anyone – while Saul, picking himself up off the ground, found himself stone-blind. They had to take him by the hand and lead him into Damascus. He continued blind for three days. He ate nothing, drank nothing."

Acts 9:3-9, as written in *The Good News Bible*: "As Saul was coming near the city of Damascus, suddenly a light from the sky flashed around him. He fell to the ground and heard a voice saying to him, 'Saul, Saul! Why do you persecute me?' 'Who are you, Lord?' he asked. 'I am Jesus, whom you persecute,' the voice said. 'But get up and go into the city, where you will be told what you must do' The men who were traveling with Saul had stopped, not saying a word; they heard the voice but could not see anyone. Saul got up from the ground and opened his eyes, but could not see a thing. So they took him by the hand and led him into Damascus. For three days he was not able to see, and during that time he did not eat or drink anything."

Acts 9:3-9, as written in *The Living Bible*: "As he was nearing Damascus on this mission, suddenly a brilliant light from heaven spotted down upon him! He fell to the ground and heard a voice saying to him, 'Paul! Paul! Why are you persecuting me?' 'Who is speaking, sir?' Paul asked. And the voice replied, 'I am Jesus, the one you are persecuting! Now get up and go into the city and await my further instructions.' The men with Paul stood speechless with surprise for they heard the sound of someone's voice but saw no one! As Paul picked himself up off the ground, he found that he was blind. He had to be led into Damascus and was there three days, blind, going without food and water all that time."

Acts 9:3-9, as written in *The New Oxford Annotated Bible* (*NRSV*): "Now as he was going along and approaching Damascus, suddenly a light from heaven flashed around him. He fell to the ground and heard a voice saying to him, 'Saul, Saul, why do you persecute me?' He asked, 'Who are you, Lord?' The reply came, 'I am Jesus, whom you are persecuting. But get up and enter the city, and you will be told what you are to do.' The men who were traveling with him stood speechless because they heard the voice but saw no one. Saul got up from the ground, and though his eyes were open, he could see nothing; so they led him by the hand and brought him into Damascus. For three days he was without sight, and neither ate nor drank."

The footnote for verse 2 explains that "The Way" was one of the earliest names for Christianity. It states, "Those who belonged to it [The Way] at Damascus were probably from Jerusalem; the empire granted the Jews the right to extradite offenders."

The footnote for verse 3 says, "The glory of God (or Christ) is often described as light."

The footnote for verses 4-5 explains the "In persecuting the disciples, he persecuted Jesus."

And the footnote for verse 7 states, "The Greek suggests that his companions heard the sound of the voice but not the words spoken."

Acts 9:3-9, as written in *TouchPoint Bible*: "As he was nearing Damascus on this mission, a brilliant light from heaven suddenly beamed down upon him! He fell to the ground and heard a voice saying to him, 'Saul! Saul! Why are you persecuting me?' 'Who are you, sir?' Saul asked. And the voice replied, 'I am Jesus, the one you are persecuting! Now get up and go into the city and you will be told what you are to do.' The men with Saul stood speechless with surprise, for they heard the sound of someone's voice, but they saw no one! As Saul picked himself up off the ground, he found that he was blind. So his companions led him by the hand to Damascus. He remained there blind for three days. And all the time he went without food and water."

Here, Saul asks, "Who are you?" In other versions, he addresses the voice as "Lord" or "Master." When he says, "Lord" is he recognizing the voice as that of Jesus?

***The Acts of the Apostles, Revised Edition*, by William Barclay, 1976, pages 70-71 and 164-165:** Barclay gives interesting details in his commentary of Acts. Barclay speculates that the persecution of the Christians in Jerusalem was preying on Saul's mind and he wanted to do more. Therefore, Saul went to the Sanhedrin to request letters of introduction to take to the synagogues in Damascus so he could hunt down Jesus followers and return them to Jerusalem in chains.

It was a trip of 140 miles, which on foot, would have taken a week. Saul was a Pharisee and, therefore, would not have had anything to do with the officers of the Sanhedrin, his only companions on the trip. In fact, he probably walked some distance from those officers.

In Acts 22:1-10, Paul tells the High Priest Ananias and the Sanhedrin about the incident. On pages 164-165 of his Acts commentary, Barclay points out how audacious it was of Paul to speak as he did before the Sanhedrin. Instead of addressing the Sanhedrin with the words, "Rulers of the people and elders of Israel," Paul called them "Brethren" insinuating that he was one of their peers. Paul didn't stop there, though. Ananias ordered the guards to slap Paul. Paul pointed out that Ananias had broken the law because it stated, "He who strikes the cheek of an Israelite, strikes, as it were, the glory of God."

Barclay explains that when Paul calls Ananias "a white-washed wall" he was essentially calling him a white-washed tomb. Since Israelites believed they were defiled if they touched a dead body, burial tombs were painted white. What Paul was really saying about Ananias was that he didn't know someone as corrupt and criminal as Ananias was known to be could be a high priest.

There were Sadducees and Pharisees on the Sanhedrin. Those two groups were at odds over many religious beliefs. As Barclay writes, "The Pharisees believed in the minutiae of the oral Law; the Sadducees accepted only the written Law.... Above all, the Pharisees believed in the resurrection of the dead; the Sadducees did not."

When Paul claimed to be a Sadducee, he was actually on trial "for the hope of resurrection from the dead." The two opposing sides of the Sanhedrin then became so violent that the commander removed Paul from the court and took him to the barracks for safety.

There was never any doubt in Paul's mind that Jesus had spoken to him out of the blinding light and that Jesus was the Messiah. His new faith emboldened him to speak with confidence and authority to Ananias and the Sanhedrin.

My thoughts: When I think about Paul, I tend to just think about all his missionary trips, his times in prison for preaching about Jesus Christ, and the many letters he wrote to instruct and encourage Christians in various locations. I can't imagine the New Testament without Paul's letters. But I seldom reflect on Paul's conversion on the road to Damascus. It is astounding to think about how determined he was to destroy the church! He was on his way to Damascus to arrest the men and women who believed in Jesus Christ. He planned to take them to Jerusalem to be tried.

I must admit that until I read Barclay's comments about Paul's confrontation with the Sanhedrin after his conversion, I didn't remember ever knowing about that violent incident.

I often say that taking a fiction writing course in 2001 was life changing for me, but my "life-changing" experience pales in comparison to Saul's conversion on the road to Damascus. Saul made a 180-degree turn, became known as Paul, and went from tracking down Christians to working tirelessly to tell people that Jesus Christ was truly the Son of God.

Am I as courageous as Paul? If brought before an anti-Christ court, confronted, and physically abused by the court, would I speak out as boldly as Paul? I hope I would, but I guess none of us know how we'll react until we're in that situation.

Is Jesus calling me by name and instructing me to go and I will be told what to do? Yes, I believe he calls each of us by name and tries to guide us and direct our lives. But I'm guilty of not listening. I let the noise of life drown out God's voice. I like to go my own way and do what I want to do. I think I know what to do with my life, but do I?

I'm good at convincing myself that God's plan for my life aligns with what I want to do. Often, I don't seek God's will until things start falling apart. It's only when I'm at my wit's end, confused and/or scared that I stop and ask God to tell me what He wants me to do.

Remember: If God can turn Saul's life around, He can turn mine around, too.

Thought Pattern Interrupter: It won't be cold forever.

Activity Suggestion: Visit a public library. Find a place to sit and read. While you're there, watch the people and listen to the excited children. (Just casually watch. Don't stare.)

See recipe for Lasagna Soup on the next page.

Comfort Recipe: Lasagna Soup

- 1 pound ground beef

- 1 (26-oz.) jar spaghetti sauce

- 1 tablespoon Italian seasoning

- 6-8 cups chicken broth

- 1 (28-oz.) can diced tomatoes, undrained

- 10 lasagna noodles, broken up

- Ricotta cheese, for garnish

- Shredded parmesan cheese, for garnish

Brown the ground beef in a soup pot and pour off excess grease. Add spaghetti sauce, Italian seasoning, and six cups of chicken broth. Add diced tomatoes. Cook for 40 minutes.

Add broken lasagna pasta pieces and cook until pasta is done. Add additional chicken broth as needed for desired consistency.

Serve in soup bowls. Top with a spoonful of ricotta cheese. Sprinkle with parmesan cheese.

Makes: A lot!

Let Light Shine Out of Darkness

Scripture for this week: II Corinthians 4:1-6

Setting the stage: Paul wrote this second letter to the church in Corinth during a difficult time. His relationship with the congregation there was not good. Apparently, some of the church members had spoken out strongly against Paul. In II Corinthians 4, Paul encourages the people not to give up.

II Corinthians 4:1-6, as written in *The Message*: "Since God has so generously let us in on what he is doing, we're not about to throw up our hands and walk off the job just because we run into occasional hard times. We refuse to wear masks and play games. We don't maneuver and manipulate behind the scenes. And we don't twist God's Word to suit ourselves. Rather, we keep everything we do and say out in the open, the whole truth on display, so that those who want to can see and judge for themselves in the presence of God. If our Message is obscure to anyone, it's not because we're holding back in any way. No, it's because these other people are looking or going the wrong way and refuse to give it serious attention. All they have eyes for is the fashionable god of darkness. They think he can give them what they want, and that they won't have to bother believing a Truth they can't see. They're stone-blind to the dayspring brightness of the Message that shines with Christ, who gives us the best picture of God we'll ever get. Remember, our Message is not about ourselves; we're proclaiming Jesus Christ, the Master. All we are is messengers, errand runners from Jesus for you. It started when God said, 'Light up the darkness!' and our lives filled up with light as we saw and understood God in the face of Christ, all bright and beautiful.

"If you only look at us, you might well miss the brightness. We carry this precious Message around in the unadorned clay pots of our ordinary lives. That's to prevent anyone from confusing God's incomparable power with us."

II Corinthians 4:1-6, as written in *The Good News Bible*: "God in his mercy has given us this work to do, and so we do not become discouraged. We put aside all secret and shameful deeds; we do not act with deceit, nor do we falsify the word of God. In the full light of truth we live in God's sight and try to commend ourselves to everyone's good conscience. For if the gospel we preach is hidden, it is hidden only from those who are being lost. They do not believe, because their minds have been kept in the dark by the evil god of this world. He keeps them from seeing the light shining on them, the light that comes from the Good News about the glory of Christ, who is the exact likeness of God. For it is not ourselves that we preach; we preach Jesus Christ as Lord, and ourselves as your servants for Jesus' sake. The

God who said, 'Out of darkness the light shall shine!' is the same God who made his light shine in our hearts, to bring us the knowledge of God's glory shining in the face of Christ.

"Yet we who have this spiritual treasure are like common clay pots, in order to show that the supreme power belongs to God, not to us."

The footnote refers us to Genesis 1:3. You may recall that Genesis 1:3 was the Scripture we looked at in Week 1.

II Corinthians 4:1-6, as written in *The Living Bible*: "It is God himself, in his mercy, who has given us this wonderful work [of telling his Good News to others], so we never give up. We do not try to trick people into believing – we are not interested in fooling anyone. We never try to get anyone to believe that the Bible teaches what it doesn't. All such shameful methods we forego. We stand in the presence of God as we speak and so we tell the truth, as all who know us will agree.

"If the Good News we preach is hidden to anyone, it is hidden from the one who is on the road to eternal death. Satan, who is the god of this evil world, has made him blind, unable to see the glorious light of the Gospel that is shining upon him, or to understand the amazing message we preach about the glory of Christ, who is God. We don't go around preaching about ourselves, but about Christ Jesus as Lord. All we say of ourselves is that we are your slaves because of what Jesus has done for us. For God, who said, 'Let there be light in the darkness,' has made us understand that it is the brightness of his glory that is seen in the face of Jesus Christ.

"But this precious treasure – this light and power that now shine within us – is held in a perishable container, that is, in our weak bodies. Everyone can see that the glorious power within must be from God and not our own."

II Corinthians 4:1-6, as written in *The New Oxford Annotated Bible (NRSV)*: "Therefore, since it is by God's mercy that we are engaged in this ministry, we do not lose heart. We have renounced the shameful things that one hides; we refuse to practice cunning or to falsify God's word; but by the open statement of the truth we commend ourselves to the conscience of everyone in the sight of God. And even if our gospel is veiled, it is veiled to those who are perishing. In their case the god of this world has blinded the minds of the unbelievers to keep them from seeing the light of the gospel of the glory of Christ, who is the image of God. For we do not proclaim ourselves; we proclaim Jesus Christ as Lord and ourselves as your slaves for Jesus' sake. For it is the God who said, 'Let light shine out of darkness,' who has shone in our hearts to give the light of the knowledge of the glory of God in the face of Jesus Christ.

"But we have this treasure in clay jars, so that it may be made clear that this extraordinary power belongs to God and does not come from us."

The footnote for verse 3 says, "Paul has apparently been accused of not making the gospel clear. The clay jars mentioned in verse 7 refer to the weakness of the body and the limitations humans have."

II Corinthians 4:1-6, as written in *TouchPoint Bible*: "And so, since God in his mercy has given us this wonderful ministry, we never give up. We reject all shameful and underhanded methods. We do not try to trick anyone, and we do not distort the word of God. We tell the truth before God, and all who are honest know that.

"If the Good News we preach is veiled from anyone, it is a sign that they are perishing. Satan, the god of this evil world, has blinded the minds of those who don't believe, so they are unable to see the glorious light of the Good News that is shining upon them. They don't understand the message we preach about the glory of Christ, who is the exact likeness of God.

"We don't go around preaching about ourselves; we preach Christ Jesus, the Lord. All we say about ourselves is that we are your servants because of what Jesus has done for us. For God, who said, 'Let there be light in the darkness,' has made us understand that this light is the brightness of the glory of God that is seen in the face of Jesus Christ.

"But this precious treasure – this light and power that now shine within us – is held in perishable containers, that is, in our weak bodies."

The footnote for verse 7 indicates that in the Greek, it says, "But we have this treasure in earthen vessels."

The Letters to the Corinthians, Revised Edition, by William Barclay, pages 195-197: In this Corinthians commentary, Barclay points out that Paul is saying something about four people or four sets of people. Paul starts by talking about himself, the task he has been given, and that he has been shone mercy. Then, Paul implies that he has enemies who have lied about him and accused him of using underhanded methods.

Paul then talks about the people who have rejected Jesus Christ. He says Satan has deafened them to the Gospel. God has not abandoned those people. The forces of evil in the world have led them astray to such a degree that they no longer hear God inviting them to accept and believe in Him.

The fourth person Paul talks about in II Corinthians 4:1-6 is Jesus Christ. He explains "that in Jesus Christ we see what God is like." This brings to mind John 14:9 in which Jesus said, "'He who has seen me has seen the Father.'" Paul is telling the Corinthians – and you and me

– that the glory of God came to earth in the form of a man – Jesus Christ.

My thoughts: What are we to take away from II Corinthians 4:1-6? God's Light shines through the life of Jesus Christ and, as Jesus followers, that same Light shines through us.

Just as I need the light of the daytime to alleviate the Seasonal Affective Disorder I experience in the fall and winter, I need to remember that the Light of God through my Savior, Jesus Christ, shines through me. I am a messenger or errand runner for Jesus when I let His Light shine in my life and my face. It shines when I treat others the way Jesus has blessed me every day of my life. Conversely, when I mistreat others, I am not reflecting God's Light.

Remember: Never give up when you're doing God's will.

Thought Pattern Interrupter: I will find something to smile about today.

Activity Suggestion: Buy yourself a box of chocolates. Just because.

Comfort Recipe: Fish Stew
- 1 large onion, roughly chopped

- 1 pound 3 ounces potatoes, cut in small chunks

- 1¼ cups chopped celery

- A little more than 1 cup ketchup

- 5 ounces tomato juice

- 1 pound deboned, skinless fish such as cod or pollock (NOT shellfish)

- ¾ teaspoon salt

- 2 teaspoons sugar

- ¼ teaspoon thyme

- ¼ teaspoon sage

- 1/8 teaspoon oregano

- Sprinkle ground ginger

- 1 small bay leaf

Cut up vegetables. Put vegetables into a soup or stock pot. Cover vegetables with water and bring to a boil along with seasonings until potatoes are tender.

In a separate pot, cover fish with water. Bring to a boil. Turn down heat and simmer until fish is cooked. Add fish and fish broth (water you cooked the fish in) to the soup pot. Simmer, but do not boil. When foam starts forming on top, the stew is ready.

Yield: 2-3 quarts

We Don't Belong to the Darkness

Scripture for this week: I Thessalonians 5:5

Setting the stage: In his first letter to the Christians in Thessalonica, Paul wanted to put their minds at ease about the second coming of Christ. He told them in I Thessalonians chapter 4 that those who believed in Jesus Christ would spend eternity in heaven.

I Thessalonians 5:5, as written in *The Message*: "But friends, you're not in the dark, so how could you be taken off guard by any of this? You're sons of Light, daughters of Day. We live under wide open skies and know where we stand."

I Thessalonians 5:5, as written in *The Good News Bible*: "But you, brothers, are not in the darkness, and the Day should not take you by surprise like a thief. All of you are people who belong to the light, who belong to the day. We do not belong to the night or to the darkness."

I Thessalonians 5:5, as written in *The Living Bible*: "But dear brothers, you are not in the dark about these things, and you won't be surprised as by a thief when that day of the Lord comes. For you are all children of the light and of the day, and do not belong to darkness and night."

I Thessalonians 5:5, as written in *The New Oxford Annotated Bible (NRSV)*: "But you, beloved, are not in darkness, for that day to surprise you like a thief; for you are all children of light and children of the day; we are not of the night or of darkness."

I Thessalonians 5:5, as written in *TouchPoint Bible*: "But you aren't in the dark about these things, dear brothers and sisters, and you won't be surprised when the day of the Lord comes like a thief. For you are children of the light and of the day; we don't belong to darkness and night."

***The Letters to the Philippians, Colossians, and Thessalonians Revised Edition*, by William Barclay, (1975) pages 204-206:** Barclay explains that the Jews believed that time was divided into two parts: (1) the present age – which was all bad and (2) the golden age of God. They believed that between the two ages was the Day of the Lord. They believed the Day of the Lord would be a terrible day. It was this Old Testament belief system that the Christians at Thessalonica had grown up with. In the fifth chapter of I Thessalonians, Paul was reminding them that as Christians they had nothing to fear about the

Day of the Lord because although they didn't know when that day was coming, they knew they'd be joining God in heaven.

Barclay states on pages 205-206: "The Christian lives in the light and no matter when that day comes, if he is watchful and sober, it will find him ready. Waking or sleeping, the Christian is living already with Christ and is therefore always prepared.... The man who has lived all his life with Christ is never unprepared to enter his nearer presence."

My thoughts: I think the takeaway from these verses is that although we don't know when we're going to die or when Jesus Christ is returning, as Christians we known where we're going and there is nothing to fear.

Remember: As Christians we have nothing to fear.

Thought Pattern Interrupter: I don't have to be perfect. Only Jesus is perfect.

Activity Suggestion: If you're able to travel, plan a day trip so you'll be prepared to take advantage of the first warm day. If you are unable to travel, think back over the places you've been and the good times you've had. Sometimes just watching a travel show on PBS can be a blessing.

See the recipe for Cherry Crisp on the next page.

Comfort Recipe: Cherry Crisp

- 1 cup uncooked oatmeal

- ½ cup all-purpose flour

- 1 cup brown sugar, lightly packed

- ½ cup nonfat dry milk (used in dry form)

- ½ cup margarine

- 1 (21-oz.) can cherry pie filling

Preheat oven to 350 degrees. Grease an 8-inch square baking pan. Mix the four dry ingredients in a bowl. Cut the margarine into the dry ingredients with a fork or pastry blender until crumbly. Put half the oatmeal mixture in the greased baking pan. Spoon a can of cherry pie filling over the oatmeal mixture in the pan. Top with the remainder of the oatmeal mixture. Bake 40 minutes or until top is brown. Serve warm with vanilla ice cream or whipped cream.

Brought Life and Immortality to Light Through the Gospel

Scripture for this week: II Timothy 1:10

Setting the stage: According to H.H. Halley in his book, *Halley's Bible Handbook, Special Abridged Edition, 1964,* Paul wrote this epistle while in prison waiting to be executed, about 66 or 67 A.D. It was in the wake of Nero's cruel and inhumane persecution of Christians around Rome that Paul found himself in prison for the last time, on what today we would call death row.

Paul's second letter to Timothy is his last known writing. He was passing the mantle on to Timothy, who was a leader in the church in Ephesus.

II Timothy 1:10, as written in *The Message*: "Since the appearance of our Savior, nothing could be plainer: death defeated, life vindicated in the steady blaze of light all through the work of Jesus."

II Timothy 1:10, as written in *The Good News Bible*: "... but now it has been revealed to us through the coming of our Savior, Christ Jesus. He has ended the power of death and through the gospel has revealed immortal life."

II Timothy 1:10, as written in *The Living Bible*: "And now he has made all of this plain to us by the coming of our Savior Jesus Christ, who broke the power of death and showed us the way of everlasting life through trusting him."

II Timothy 1:10, as written in *The New Oxford Annotated Bible (NRSV)*: "... but it has now been revealed through the appearing of our Savior Christ Jesus, who abolished death and brought life and immortality to light through the gospel."

II Timothy 1:10, as written in *TouchPoint Bible*: "And now he has made all of this plain to us by the coming of Christ Jesus, our Savior, who broke the power of death and showed us the way to everlasting life through the Good News."

***The Letters to Timothy, Titus, and Philemon, Revised Edition, by William Barclay, (1975) pages 145-148*:** Barclay gives II Timothy 1:8-11 the title, "A Gospel Worth Suffering For." In those verses Paul calls us to not be ashamed to bear witness to the Lord and to accept the suffering which the Gospel brings.

Paul was a prisoner in Rome when he wrote this letter to Timothy. In it he presents "the sheer grandeur of the Gospel." Barclay sets the stage for this letter when he states, "To the ancient world the gospel was the power to live. That very age in which Paul was writing was the great age of suicide. The highest-principled of the ancient thinkers were the Stoics; but they had their own way out when life became intolerable."

The Stoics believed that God gave people the power to take their own lives. This was a belief system that existed when Paul was writing Timothy; hence, Paul emphasized that the Gospel is power – power to keep living when you feel like you just can't go on.

Barclay says in addition to power, the Gospel is salvation, consecration, grace, life and immortality, service, and God's purpose.

My thoughts: In this week's Scripture passage, Paul tells us to accept the suffering the Gospel brings on us. I am blessed. I am an American and I have never suffered for my Christian faith. It is difficult for me to imagine suffering for believing in Jesus Christ, but I know that Christians in many parts of the world have suffered and suffer today for their beliefs.

What jumped out at me in Barclay's explanation above is the part about the belief of Stoics that suicide was acceptable and that is why Paul emphasized the power of the Gospel to give us the power to keep living in spite of our circumstances. Even when we feel like we can't go on. How many times have you felt like you couldn't go on?

I'm not talking about suicide here. I'm thinking about the times I did not have the energy to put one foot in front of the other. I'm thinking about the times I didn't have the energy to feed myself.

You might have noticed that only two of the five versions of II Timothy 1:10 used the word "light." I considered omitting this week's devotional for that reason; however, after re-reading Barclay's interpretation about the power of the Gospel to empower us when we feel like we can't go on, I decided to leave it in this book. If you have chronic fatigue syndrome, fibromyalgia, or any one of a multitude of other chronic and debilitating or isolating illnesses, you know what I'm talking about.

Remember: Jesus Christ conquered death so we don't have to fear it.

Thought Pattern Interrupter: Winter is just a season. Spring will come again.

Activity Suggestion: Start going through your warm weather clothes, and doing what you can to get into shape so you can wear them and be comfortable in them. I'm not "body shaming" here. Many of us gain weight over the winter when we tend to not get as much exercise as we do during the warmer months. Spring is a good time to evaluate what you can do to improve your health.

Comfort Recipe: Joan's Chicken Pie

I don't know who Joan was, but this is a recipe my mother copied from a TV cooking show many years ago. It's always a hit!

- 1½ pounds boneless, skinless chicken breasts

- 1 (15-oz.) can mixed vegetables, drained (or 2 cups of frozen mixed vegetables, thawed)

- 1 (11-oz.) can cream of celery soup

- 1 (11-oz.) can cream of mushroom soup

- 1 (11-oz.) can cream of chicken soup

- 1 cup self-rising flour

- 1 cup milk

- 2 sticks margarine, melted (or less, to make it healthier)

Cook chicken breasts and cut or shred into bite-size pieces.

Lightly spray 9x13-inch baking dish with cooking spray. Spread chicken pieces in the dish. Layer and spread each of the following ingredients in order listed over the chicken: celery soup, mixed vegetables (drained), mushroom soup, and chicken soup.

In a bowl, whisk together melted margarine, flour, and milk. Pour over ingredients in the baking dish, but do not stir.

Bake at 375 degrees for 1 hour.

Yield: 8 servings

Chosen People... Out of Darkness into a Wonderful Light

Scripture for this week: I Peter 2:9-10

Setting the stage: Peter wrote his two epistles to the churches in Asia Minor during the time of Nero's persecution of Christians around Rome.

I think I studied Asia Minor in the fifth grade, but that was more than 60 years ago. To refresh my memory, I looked it up. In case you're in the same boat, I'll share what I found.

Asia Minor is a peninsula in western Asia that forms most of modern day Turkey. It is bordered by the Aegean Sea, the Black Sea, and the Mediterranean Sea.

Now that we have our bearings, let's look at this week's Scripture.

I Peter 2:9-10, as written in *The Message*: "But you are the ones chosen by God, chosen for the high calling of priestly work, chosen to be a holy people, God's instruments to do his work and speak out for him, to tell others of the night-and-day difference he made for you – from nothing to something, from rejected to accepted."

I Peter 2:9-10, as written in *The Good News Bible*: "But you are the chosen race, the King's priests, the holy nation, God's own people, chosen to proclaim the wonderful acts of God, who called you out of darkness into his own marvelous light. At one time you were not God's people; at one time you did not know God's mercy, but now you have received his mercy."

I Peter 2:9-10, as written in *The Living Bible*: "But you are not like that, for you have been chosen by God himself – you are priests of the King, you are holy and pure, you are God's very own – all this so that you may show to others how God called you out of the darkness into his wonderful light. Once you were less than nothing; now you are God's own. Once you knew very little of God's kindness; now your very lives have been changed by it."

I Peter 2:9-10, as written in *The New Oxford Annotated Bible (NRSV)*: "But you are a chosen race, a royal priesthood, a holy nation, God's own people, in order that you may proclaim the mighty acts of him who called you out of darkness into his marvelous light. Once you were not a people, but now you are God's people; once you had not received mercy, but now you have received mercy."

I Peter 2:9-10, as written in *TouchPoint Bible*: "But you are not like that, for you are a chosen people. You are a kingdom of priests.

God's holy nation, his very own possession. This is so you can show others the goodness of God, for he called you out of the darkness into his wonderful light."

Verse 10 is inspired by Hosea 1:6, 9; and 2:23. Verse 10 states: "Once you were not a people; now you are the people of God. Once you received none of God's mercy; now you have received his mercy."

***The Letters of James and Peter, Revised Edition*, by William Barclay, (1976) pages 193-199:** Barclay writes extensively about "The Nature and Function of the Church, "which is what he calls I Peter 2:4-10. He states, "A very ordinary thing acquires a new value, if it has been possessed by some famous person.... It is so with the Christian. The Christian may be a very ordinary person but he acquires a new value because he belongs to God."

Remember: You belong to God, and He will never forsake you or give up on you.

Thought Pattern Interrupter: I was made in God's image.

Activity Suggestion: Call that nursing home again that you called in Week 5. If they didn't need anything then, they might now.

See recipe for Slow Cooker Hamburger and Barley Soup on the next page.

Comfort Recipe: Slow Cooker Hamburger and Barley Soup

This is one of my favorite winter soups!

- ¾ pound ground beef

- 1 onion, chopped

- 1 (28-oz.) carton beef broth

- 1¾ cups water

- 2 teaspoons beef bouillon powder

- 1 (28-oz.) can diced tomatoes

- 3 carrots, sliced

- 3 celery ribs, sliced

- ½ cup pearled barley

- 1 bay leaf

- 1 teaspoon dried thyme

- 1 T. dried parsley

- ½ teaspoon black pepper

Brown ground beef and onion in skillet. Drain excess grease. Combine all ingredients in slow cooker. Cover. Cook on low for 6 or more hours or on high for 3 hours. Freezes well. Yield: 10 cups

Every Perfect Gift... From the Father of Light and lights

S cripture for this week: James 1:16-17

Setting the stage: James is remembered for his stance on faith and works. James emphasized a Christian's obligation to take care of the poor and suffering people.

James 1:16-17, as written in *The Message*: "So, my very dear friends, don't get thrown off course. Every desirable and beneficial gift comes out of heaven. The gifts are rivers of light cascading down from the Father of Light."

James 1:16-17, as written in *The Good News Bible*: "Do not be deceived, my dear brothers! Every good gift and every perfect present comes from heaven; it comes down from God, the Creator of the heavenly lights, who does not change or cause darkness by turning."

James 1:16-17, as written in *The Living Bible*: "So don't be misled, dear brothers. But whatever is good and perfect comes to us from God, the Creator of all light, and he shines forever without change or shadow."

James 1:16-17, as written in *The New Oxford Annotated Bible (NRSV)*: "Do not be deceived, my beloved. Every generous act of giving, with every perfect gift, is from above, coming down from the Father of lights, with whom there is no variation or shadow due to change."

James 1:16-17, as written in *TouchPoint Bible*: "So don't be misled, my dear brothers and sisters. Whatever is good and perfect comes to us from God above, who created all heaven's lights. Unlike them, he never changes or casts shifting shadows."

***The Letters of James and Peter, Revised Edition*, by William Barclay, (1976) page 54:** Barclay says James is stressing "The unchangeableness of God." The lights God created – the sun, the moon, the stars – vary in the light they give, "but he who created them never changes."

Remember: The Creator of light never changes.

Thought Pattern Interrupter: Today is the day God gave me. I will rejoice!

Activity Suggestion: Invite someone for soup.

Comfort Recipe: Easy Chicken Noodle Soup

- 2 boneless, skinless chicken breasts, cooked and chopped or shredded

- 5 cups chicken broth

- 10 cups water

- 2 tablespoons olive oil to saute vegetables (do not use butter)

- 1 onion, finely chopped

- 3 carrots, either sliced or grated

- 2 celery ribs, chopped or thinly-sliced

- ½ pound spiral pasta such as rotini

- Salt to taste

Put 10 cups of water and 5 cups of chicken broth in a stock pot and heat on medium-high.

While the liquids are heating, saute onion in olive oil in a skillet. When onions have softened, increase heat to medium-high and add carrots and celery. Add more oil, if needed. Saute, stirring often until vegetables are soft and golden brown, then add to soup pot. Add cooked chicken. Bring to a low boil.

Add pasta and continue cooking for about 15 minutes or until pasta is desired softness. Season to taste.

Yield: 8 to 10 servings. Due to the pasta, this soup does not freeze well.

If We Walk in Light,... Christ... Cleans Us from All Sin

Scripture for this week: I John 1:5

Setting the stage: This epistle is thought to have been written by the apostle John perhaps as a letter to circulate among the churches around Ephesus. The statement made in I John 1:5 is so simple, yet profound, that its wording is almost identical in every version of the Bible that I read.

I John 1:5, as written in *The Message*: "This, in essence, is the message we heard from Christ and are passing on to you.: God is light, pure light; there's not a trace of darkness in him."

I John 1:5, as written in *The Good News Bible*: "Now the message that we have heard from his Son and announce is this: God is light, and there is no darkness at all in him."

I John 1:5, as written in *The Living Bible*: "This is the message God has given us to pass on to you: that God is Light and in him is no darkness at all."

I John 1:5, as written in *The New Oxford Annotated Bible (NRSV)*: "This is the message we have heard from him and proclaim to you, that God is light and in him there is no darkness at all.

I John 1:5, as written in *TouchPoint Bible*: "This is the message he has given us to announce to you: God is light and there is no darkness in him at all."

***The Letters of John and Jude, Revised Edition*, (1975) by William Barclay, (1976) page 25:** Barclay begins his comments about this verse by stating a thought that had never occurred to me: "A man's character will necessarily be determined by the character of the god whom he worships; and, therefore, John begins by laying down the nature of the God and Father of Jesus Christ whom Christians worship."

Barclay then begins to unpack what the statement made – the fact laid out – in verse 5 means. He says verse 5 tells us of God's "sheer splendour." It tells us there is nothing secretive about God, that God is pure, that God offers to guide us, and that God's presence reveals "the imperfections of life."

Barclay goes on to explain darkness in the context of the New Testament. He states, "Throughout the New Testament darkness stands for the very opposite of the Christian life." We live in darkness until we know Jesus Christ.

Darkness tries to overcome the light but it can't – and it never will.

The fruits of the Holy Spirit (love, joy, peace, longsuffering, gentleness, goodness, faith, meekness, and temperance) will not grow without the Light of Christ.

Darkness is life separated from God.

Remember: God is pure Light. God has no darkness.

Thought Pattern Interrupter: Spring is coming!

Activity Suggestion: Call a local Ronald McDonald House or other such facility and ask what they need. A batch of cookies? Paper products? Toiletries? Pre-packaged snack food? (They might have rules about donating home-baked goods, so be sure to inquire about that in advance.)

See the recipe for Double Fudge Pudding on the next page.

Comfort Recipe: Double Fudge Pudding

- 1 cup all-purpose flour

- 2 teaspoons baking soda

- ¾ cup sugar

- 2 tablespoons cocoa

- ½ teaspoon salt

- ½ cup milk

- 1 teaspoon vanilla

- 2 tablespoons shortening, melted

- ¾ to 1 cup chopped pecans, optional

To pour on top:

- ¾ cup brown sugar

- ¼ cup cocoa

- 2 cups hot water

Sift together first 5 dry ingredients. Add milk, vanilla, and melted shortening. Mix until smooth. Add pecans, if desired. Pour into greased 8x12x2-inch baking pan.

Mix brown sugar and ¼ cup cocoa and sprinkle over batter. Pour hot water over entire batter. Bake at 350 degrees for 30 minutes. The cake batter will rise to the top and the liquid on top will form a sauce on the bottom.

Serve warm with whipped cream or vanilla ice cream.

God is Light

Setting the stage: This week we pick up with the four verses that follow the verse we looked at last week. Feel free to turn back a few pages and review I John 1:5.

Verses 6-9 in the first letter of John address the joys of living in God's Light and the consequences of ignoring it.

I John 1:6-10, as written in *The Message*: "If we claim that we experience a shared life with him and continue to stumble around in the dark, we're obviously lying through our teeth – we're not living what we claim. But if we walk in the light, God himself being the light, we also experience a shared life with one another, as the sacrificed blood of Jesus, God's Son, purges all our sin. If we claim that we're free of sin, we're only fooling ourselves. A claim like that is errant nonsense. On the other hand, if we admit our sins – simply come clean about them – he won't let us down: he'll be true to himself. He'll forgive our sins and purge us of all wrongdoing. If we claim that we've never sinned, we out-and-out contradict God — make a liar out of him. A claim like that only shows off our ignorance of God."

I John 1:6-10, as written in *The Good News Bible*: "If, then, we say that we have fellowship with him, yet at the same time live in the darkness we are lying both in our words and in our actions. But if we live in the light -- just as he is in the light – then we have fellowship with one another, and the blood of Jesus, his Son, purifies us from every sin. If we say that we have no sin, we deceive ourselves, and there is no truth in us. But if we confess our sins to God, he will keep his promises and do what is right: he will forgive us our sins and purify us from all our wrongdoing. If we say that we have not sinned, we make a liar out of God, and his word is not in us."

I John 1:6-10, as written in *The Living Bible*: "So if we say we are his friends, but go on living in spiritual darkness and sin, we are lying. But if we are living in the light of God's presence, just as Christ does, then we have wonderful fellowship and joy with each other, and the blood of Jesus his Son cleanses us from every sin. If we say we have no sin, we are only fooling ourselves, and refusing to accept the truth. But if we confess our sins to him, he can be depended on to forgive us and to cleanse us from every wrong. [And it is perfectly proper for God to do this for us because Christ died to wash away our sins.] If we claim we have not sinned, we are lying and calling God a liar, for he says we have sinned."

I John 1:6-10, as written in *The New Oxford Annotated Bible (NRSV)*: "If we say that we have fellowship with him while we are walking in darkness we lie and do not do what is true; but if we walk in the light as he himself is in the light, we have fellowship with one another, and the blood of Jesus his Son cleanses us from all sin. If we say that we have no sin, we deceive ourselves, and the truth is not in us. If we confess our sins, he who is faithful and just will forgive us our sins and cleanse us from all unrighteousness. If we say that we have not sinned, we make him a liar, and his word is not in us."

The footnote says that the phrase "walking in darkness" refers to "habitual and intentional evil conduct."

I John 1:6-10, as written in *TouchPoint Bible*: "So we are lying if we say we have fellowship with God but go on living in spiritual darkness. We are not living in the truth. But if we are living in the light of God's presence, just as Christ is, then we have fellowship with each other, and the blood of Jesus, his Son, cleanses us from every sin. If we say we have no sin, we are only fooling ourselves and refusing to accept the truth. But if we confess our sins to him, he is faithful and just to forgive us and to cleanse us from every wrong. If we claim we have not sinned, we are calling God a liar and showing that his word has no place in our hearts."

***The Letters of John and Jude, Revised Edition*, (1975) by William Barclay, (1976) pages 28-31:** In the time of John, there were those who thought they were too intellectual and spiritual to be subject to laws or the idea of sin. Barclay says that in order to have fellowship with God a person "must walk in the light." To live otherwise – "in the moral and ethical darkness" – we can't have fellowship with God.

As I stated earlier, Barclay wrote in the days before inclusive language. When he says "man" or "men," we should substitute "person" or "people."

Barclay clarifies the words in verse 7 about the blood of Jesus as follows: "The meaning is that all the time, day by day, constantly and consistently, the blood of Jesus Christ ought to be carrying out a cleansing process in the life of the individual Christian. The concept "looks at the sacrifice of Christ as something which not only atones for past sin but equips a man in holiness day by day."

Barclay makes it clear that a person who claims to be in fellowship with God but who lives at odds with those claims is a liar. Plainly stated, Barclay says, "The man who professes to love Christ and deliberately disobeys him, is guilty of a lie."

Remember: If we say that we have no sin, we deceive ourselves, and the truth is not in us. If we confess our sins, God, who is faithful and just, will forgive us our sins and cleanse us from all unrighteousness.

Thought Pattern Interrupter: If not for winter, I wouldn't appreciate spring.

Activity Suggestion: Buy some flowers, and make a list of the things you'll miss about winter. I dare you!

Comfort Recipe: Marie's Macaroni and Chicken Casserole

- 1 cup elbow macaroni

- ¾ cup milk

- 1 (11-oz.) can cream of chicken soup

- 2 cups chopped cooked chicken

- 1 cup shredded sharp cheddar cheese, divided

- ¼ cup chopped pimiento

Cook macaroni according to package directions; drain.

In a bowl, stir milk into soup. Add chicken, half the cheese, pimiento, and the cooked macaroni. Mix well.

Pour into a greased 2-quart casserole dish.

Bake, covered, at 350 degrees for 50 minutes. Uncover and stir. Top with remaining cheese; bake until cheese melts, two or three minutes longer.

Yield: 8 servings

My Prayer for You

N ow that you have made it through another autumn and winter, my prayer is that you are feeling refreshed and renewed. I pray that you are now welcoming spring and summer and perhaps a lessening of your aches and pains. I pray that the Scriptures highlighted in this devotional book have lightened your load and equipped you to face next autumn and winter with less dread and anxiety than you have in the past.

I pray that, even though the aches and pains of chronic illness might ebb and flow, you will find peace and not let your unease about the coming winter prevent you from enjoying the beauty of autumn.

I pray that you will be able to adopt my mother's often-said words to live by: Take one day at a time. That is easier said than done. I know, because I have been trying to practice that all my life. It does us no good to let tomorrow ruin today. It is not good to let our anticipation of the cold days of winter ruin the crisp and colorful days of autumn. In most of the world God has blessed us with four distinct seasons. He wants us to find joy in each of them. I pray that you will seek the support of

God the Father, God the Son, and God the Holy Spirit every day of your life. Seek God's will, accept His forgiveness and grace, and let His Light shine through you in every season of the year and every season of your life.

I pray that you have everything you need and that you live in a place of contentment. I pray that the words of Paul in the eighth chapter of Romans will give you peace.

Romans 8:38-39, as written in *The Message*: "I'm absolutely convinced that nothing — nothing living or dead, angelic or demonic, today or tomorrow, high or low, thinkable or unthinkable — absolutely nothing can get between us and God's love because of the way that Jesus our Master has embraced us."

Romans 8:38-39, as written in *The Good News Bible*: "For I am certain that nothing can separate us from his love: neither death nor life, neither angels nor other heavenly rulers or powers, neither the present nor the future, neither the world above nor the world below — there is nothing in all creation that will ever be able to separate us from the love of God which is ours through Christ Jesus our Lord."

Romans 8:38-39, as written in The Living Bible: "For I am convinced that nothing can ever separate us from his love. Death can't, and life can't. The angels won't, and all the powers of hell itself cannot keep God's love away. Our fears for today, our worries about tomorrow, or where we are — high above the sky, or in the deepest ocean — nothing will ever be able to separate us from the love of God demonstrated by our Lord Jesus Christ when he died for us."

Romans 8:38-39, as written in The New Oxford Annotated Bible (NRSV): "For I am convinced that neither death, nor life, nor angels, nor rulers, nor things present, nor things to come, nor powers, nor height, nor depth, nor anything else in all creation, will be able to separate us from the love of God in Christ Jesus our Lord."

Romans 8:38-39, as written in TouchPoint Bible: "And I am convinced that nothing can ever separate us from his love. Death can't, and life can't. Our fears for today, our worries about tomorrow, and even the powers of hell can't keep God's love away. Whether we are high above the sky or in the deepest ocean, nothing in all creation will ever be able to separate us from the love of God that is revealed in Christ Jesus our Lord."

Remember: Nothing can separate you from the love of God.

.

Recipe Index

B everages

Beth's Hot Chocolate, 91

Bread

Creamy Cornbread, 112

Easy No-Egg Cornbread, 45

Mama's Drop Biscuits, 4-5

Soups, Stews, and Chili

Black Bean Soup, 100-101

Brunswick Stew, 116

Easy Chicken Noodle Soup, 149

Fish Stew, 130-131

Lasagna Soup, 124

Presbyterian Hospital Chili, 60-61

Slow Cooker Blackeyed Pea Stew, 36

Slow Cooker Chicken Chili, 106-107

Slow Cooker Hamburger and Barley Soup, 146

Main Dishes

Aunt Della's Chicken and Rice Casserole, 28

Barbecue Stacks, 14-15

Easy Cheesy Lasagna, 20-21

Joan's Chicken Pie, 140-141

Marie's Macaroni and Chicken Casserole, 158-159

Mary Jane's Meatloaf, 9

Mexican One Dish, 74

Savory Ham and Rice, 68

Spoonburgers, 80

Desserts and Snacks

Aunt Lila Mae's Chocolate Pie, 85-86

Cherry Crisp, 136

Double Fudge Pudding, 154

Marie's Cereal Mix, 50-51

About the author

J anet Morrison grew up in Harrisburg, North Carolina. She holds a Bachelor of Arts degree in Political Science with a minor in History from Appalachian State University and a Master of Public Affairs from North Carolina State University at Raleigh. In 2001, Janet took a fiction writing course at Queens University of Charlotte. It was a life-changing course. She is a lifelong Presbyterian and comes from a long line of Presbyterians and Methodists.

Janet wrote this devotional book out of her decades of experience with Chronic Fatigue Syndrome, Fibromyalgia, and Seasonal Affective Disorder. She needs natural light in the mornings to combat Seasonal Affective Disorder, and she needs Jesus Christ — The Light of the World — to cope with all life's challenges and stresses.

In her blog, Janet's Writing Blog, Janet writes opinion pieces about current events, shares her thoughts about some of the books she reads, writes posts of historical significance on or near the anniversary dates of those events, and occasionally writes about local North Carolina history. Find her blog at https://www.janetswritingblog.com.

Her website is https://www.janetmorrisonbooks.com. By visiting her website, you can subscribe to her newsletter. By doing so, you will receive a free downloadable copy of her historical short story, "Slip Sliding Away." Here's the link:

*https://www.janetmorris
onbooks.com*

Also by Janet Morrison

As a freelance writer, Janet Morrison wrote a local history column for *Harrisburg Horizons* newspaper in Harrisburg, North Carolina, from May 2006 through 2012. In 2022 and early 2023, she published those newspaper articles in paperback and e-book with the titles *Harrisburg, Did You Know? Cabarrus History, Book 1* and *Harrisburg, Did You Know? Cabarrus History, Book 2*. Those books are available in paperback at Second Look Books in Harrisburg, NC and available in paperback and e-book from Amazon.

Her historical short story, "Slip Sliding Away" is also available in paperback and e-book from Amazon.

She published an historical ghost story, "Ghost of the Battle of Guilford Courthouse: An American Revolutionary War Ghost Story," in 2023. It is available in paperback and e-book from Amazon.

Her vintage postcard book, *The Blue Ridge Mountains of North Carolina*, was published in 2014 by Arcadia Publishing. It is available in paperback and e-book from Amazon and in paperback from Arcadia Publishing. It is occasionally available at independent bookstores in western North Carolina, or you can request that your favorite bookstore order it for you.

Janet and her sister, Marie Morrison, published a family cookbook in 2023. The title is a play on words that came from a multi-generational tradition in their family. *The Aunts in the Kitchen: Southern Family Recipes* contains recipes from all the aunts in their family. Janet and Marie are now affectionately known as "The Aunts" by their nieces and nephews. It is a moniker they claim with pride. The cookbook includes snippets of information and memories of Janet and Marie's aunts. They were all good cooks! The cookbook is available in paperback at Second Look Books in Harrisburg, NC and from Amazon.

In 1996, Janet and Marie, compiled and published three genealogy books: *Descendants of John & Mary Morrison of Rocky River*; *Descendants of James & Jennet Morrison of Rocky River*; and *Descendants of Robert & Sarah Morrison of Rocky River*. Those hardback books are available from Janet and Marie through https://www.janetmorrrisonbooks.com.

Janet hopes to publish more historical short stories. She is writing an historical novel set along the Great Wagon Road in Virginia, North Carolina, and South Carolina in the 1760s.

She thanks you for purchasing this devotional book and hopes it will bring you peace.

If you are so inclined, she would appreciate your rating or even leaving a short review of this and her other books on Amazon, Goodreads, or other online review venues. Reviews are incredibly valuable to writers, especially when they, like Janet, are trying to establish credibility and name recognition. Thank you for purchasing, reading, reviewing, and telling your friends about this book!

For book descriptions and purchasing information, visit https://www.janetmorrisonbooks.com Here is a QR code for your convenience:

Thank you for purchasing *I Need The Light: 26 Weekly Devotionals to Help You Through Winter*. Please rate the book on Goodreads, Amazon, and other places where you look for book reviews. A review would be very much appreciated, even if just a few words.

Janet's Parting Words for You

Remember: The Word of God is a lamp to your feet and light to your path.

Psalm 119:105, the Scripture from Week 2 in this devotional book, as written in *The New Oxford Annotated Bible (NRSV)*: "Your word is a lamp to my feet and a light to my path."